D1330704

LIVING WITH
HOPE

*A true story
of faith, purpose
and mobility*

MICHAEL PANTHER

10 Publishing
a division of 10 ofthose.com

British Library Cataloguing in Publication Data
A record for this book is available from the British Library

ISBN: 978-1-915705-97-6

Designed by Pete Barnsley (CreativeHoot.com)
Cover photograph by Josh Roeda

Printed in Denmark

10Publishing, a division of 10ofthose.com
Unit C, Tomlinson Road, Leyland, PR25 2DY, England

Email: info@10ofthose.com
Website: www.10ofthose.com

1 3 5 7 10 8 6 4 2

CONTENTS

FOREWORD

My first encounter with Michael Panther was at Joni and Friends while wheeling the hallways of our International Disability Center. Any time I see a wheelchair user at our Center, I like to stop and learn their story. I wasn't prepared to hear the pain yet power behind Michael's.

This winsome young man with a winning smile had come to serve in our internship program. When I asked why he wanted to be an intern, Michael was quick to share his heart for his fellow Africans who, like him, had suffered great disappointment and affliction.

That meeting when we parked our wheelchairs beside each other was years ago. Since then, Michael Panther has forged an incredible ministry far beyond what he dreamed of as an intern with Joni and Friends. For all his many challenges; for all the years he suffered through the South Sudan war; for all his incalculable losses, Michael still keeps his winning smile.

It's what makes me love Jesus more when I am around him.

And I'm happy to tell you that the book you hold in your hands will do the same. In the pages of *Living with Hope*, you'll get to know a fellow sufferer who has held fast to God and his Word through unthinkable afflictions. Here is a Christian leader whose wisdom has been honed through constant hardships. Michael writes with authority when he echoes his Lord, saying, "Do not be surprised at fiery ordeals… in this world you will have trouble… we must enter the kingdom through many tribulations." Yes, the author of this book understands suffering.

Yet Michael has cultivated a sweet humility and submission to Christ that makes God look astonishing. Through his tireless labors and constant trials, my friend has come to view challenges as his allies. In short, hardship has made Michael Panther a man of solid character.

If like me you wrestle with affliction, you will be strengthened by the insights in *Living with Hope*. You will learn that God is more interested in what you become than in what you get out of life. He is more interested in what you need than in what you want. It is a lesson God has taught me in my wheelchair, and like my friend from Africa, my disability is the bruising-of-a-blessing that has drawn me nearer to my precious Savior.

I encourage you to read the book you hold in your hands slowly and carefully. The pages are filled with winsome stories, rich insights, and practical guidance for those who are thirsty for more than this world can give. In *Living with Hope*, you will discover that your disappointments are your passport to a livelier and more earnest walk with Jesus Christ.

So, grab a cup of coffee and flip the page – by the last chapter, you'll be thanking God for *your* bruised blessings, whether they be failures, botched surgeries, the aches of aging, long-standing losses, or perhaps like me, even a fateful dive into water.

Bless you for allowing Michael Panther to be your guide as you step beyond the shallows of your faith and into deeper water. And don't be frightened if you get in above your neck... for it is in deep waters where God *always* reveals more of himself.

Joni Eareckson Tada
Joni and Friends International Disability Center
Agoura Hills, California

PROLOGUE

Shhhsp. Shhhsp. Shhhsp.

"Michael, come quickly! You have to see this."

I turn in my wheelchair and head toward the speaker, who is now pointing. I cannot believe my eyes. Before me is a woman on her hands and knees, gripping the thongs of a pair of worn-out flip-flops. Every time the flip-flops slide forward, they make the *shhhsp* sound as they scrape against the floor. She has taped a pair of worn-out kneepads to her knees, their outer shells long ago peeled away from traversing the rocky roads. Beside her walks a young girl, probably no more than three years old, who hangs on to her for dear life.

I can't help but gasp at the determination and trust of this woman in crawling her way to our clinic. Until this morning, we'd thought we had seen it all. Every sort of mobility need we could imagine had passed through our clinic doors. But when Chama crawls in on all fours, the room goes silent as all eyes turn toward her.

Chama's clothing and the blanket tied around her waist are tattered and dirty from being dragged through the grime of the city streets. Her two withered lower limbs, with feet pointing upward, hang in the air in old compression socks. She is a tall woman who has no doubt spent her life in this bowed posture, unable to look into the eyes of others. Later, we learn Chama has come from the neighboring town of Shauri Moyo, some twenty kilometers away, and where, except for her small daughter, she has been alone and unassisted.

But Living with Hope is there to help. As I look back, I realize everything in my life has led to this moment. This is what God intended for my life and began directing me toward many, many years ago.

1

LITTLE BOY LOST

I woke suddenly, my heart pounding fiercely. I sat up from the grass mat I slept on with my younger brother and sister, next to my parents. Why were people screaming outside our hut?

"Gunfire!" my father shouted when we all startled at the popping sounds.

I could smell smoke, too, but it wasn't our morning fire. Only three years old, I was terrified. "What's happening, Baba? Mama?"

My father jumped up and rushed outside. Just as quickly, my mother pushed me and my terrified siblings out of our hut and into the night.

"Hurry!"

Now my heart raced as we all fled through darkness toward the shelter of bushes and the forest beyond. I tripped over something, and in the glow of flickering light, I could see several people lying on the ground. They weren't moving. Were they dead?

"Hurry!" my mother urged over and over in a loud whisper. I couldn't resist my curiosity, though, and I glanced behind me. Men were setting the homes of our village ablaze. Some of our neighbors were still inside them, and I could hear their shrieking. Horrified, I fought back tears as we sped toward relative safety. What would happen to us?

I must have glanced back one too many times, for—amid the confusion of smoke and chaos—I suddenly realized my family was nowhere to be seen in the dark forest. I couldn't even hear their voices, and I both panicked and froze. Yet I remembered my parents' repeated instructions for such a time as this. Resisting the urge to shout for my mother, I lay low in a patch of earth free of grass as the sounds of anguish and the light of flames filtered through the trees.

Afraid to move, I stayed there for the rest of the night, awake and quiet even as the sun came up, waiting for my family to find me. When no one came, I remembered hearing my parents pray. In my own way, I cried out to their God: *Save me!*

***

I woke to the early rays of the sun sifting through the tops of the trees, the third dawn since I'd hidden myself. Too afraid to look for food or water, I'd had neither. Even if I wanted to move now, how could I? I could hardly lift my head. Tears threatened once more, and I wanted nothing more than my mother's arms around me.

Sometime later that day, footsteps crunched against the forest floor. They were coming toward me, closer and closer. As I trembled with fear, I was certain an enemy was about to end my life: *If those people killed the others, they'll kill me too.*

The footsteps stopped close to my ear. "It's all right. I'm here to help."

I looked up to see the kind face of a Dinka Bor soldier. I recognized him by the missing lower teeth and the markings on his forehead. He spoke to me in the Dinka Bor language. After giving me water and a little food, he then carried me to the safety of a makeshift camp. My parents and siblings had been waiting there, praying I'd be found and returned to them.

I'd been saved. But my life would never be the same.

Some people think trauma experienced early in a child's life is soon forgotten. "He's young. He'll get over it. There won't be any lasting impact," they say. But they are wrong. It's not true. I can assure you that trauma sears memories into the minds of young children. The trauma I suffered so early in my life lives with me yet today, and I am conscious that I must fight against the boogeyman of my fears on a daily basis.

***

When I was born in the early 1990s—around Christmastime, as my mother recalls—Sudan was embroiled in an intense civil war between the government in the North and liberation fighters in the South. The reasons for war are always complex, and they often evolve over time. Today, what began as a battle for a free South

Sudan continues among warring tribal factions, even after achieving Southern independence. At the heart of the conflict has been a struggle for power and economic resources. Innocent civilians like the members of my people group, the Dinka Bor, have been caught in the middle for decades. Mass ethnic slaughter wiped out our clans and villages.

Before decades of conflict drastically altered our way of life, our people had dwelt peacefully in the forests of the savanna lands and along the Nile River. We lived together in a community led by village elders. These chiefs oversaw clan affairs, our spiritual shepherding, and the rituals and rites of passage that preserved our culture. We were pastoralists, with our lives centering on the raising and grazing of cattle. To the Dinka, a large herd of cattle was a man's wealth, a precious possession. So valuable were our livestock that our children were named after the most prized among the herd. We were a people known for our exceptional stature and smooth, dark skin. We took great pride in our appearance, the marking on our forehead of manhood, our courage, and our tribal identity.

By the turn of the millennium, war had left us with few animals. Either they had been stolen by attacking militia or we had been forced to abandon them, leaving them to die, when the conflict required that we moved suddenly for safety. We had long set aside our rhythms of seasonal migration with our herds for mere survival farming and grazing.

After the attack on our village when I was three, my family lived on the run. We often went days without food and clean water. We grew what sorghum and millet we could, but producing crops from seed took time, and time was never guaranteed. A poor harvest during the growing season meant hunger and suffering when the dry season arrived. We foraged for roots in the forest to survive.

The rainy season brought its own despair. The land flooded, and with it came mosquitoes and the threat of malaria. We had no access to medical care or humanitarian aid. We became a people skeleton-thin with sunken eyes.

Many children died of starvation, and those who lived carried the swollen bellies of malnutrition. Few made it to their third birthdays. In those years, my mother gave birth to several more children, and we watched helplessly as two of my younger brothers died of starvation. We were devastated. Consuming my parents' thoughts was the fear that their remaining children would also succumb. They were always worried about this. When my newest sister was born, they named her *Adier*, the word for "weariness" in the Dinka language. Conflict and suffering exacted a high psychological toll. We struggled to understand the cruel effects of war that we experienced daily, and the price that it exacted from the most innocent among us.

We were frequently on the move away from conflict and toward safer ground. Many of our people began a thousand-mile journey toward refuge in neighboring Ethiopia. But for others like my clan, we became a people internally displaced, roving across Southern Sudan. At times we would shelter under trees for a few days. Then once we felt safe, we would set up camp, rebuild huts of mud and thatch, and restore some sort of normal community life. If conditions allowed it, we would stay in that location for a year or more before attempting to return to a previous village site. But eventually, the war would find us again.

We were not alone in our flight to safety. More than two million people from South Sudan have become refugees or asylum seekers. The country remains one of the poorest and most underdeveloped in the world, and severe food insecurity and conflict continue to affect vulnerable people. Hunger is everywhere, and persistent conflict, desert locust swarms, economic crisis, and flooding all increase the risk of disease and famine. Many children still die of starvation before their third birthdays, and those who remain still carry the swollen bellies of malnutrition.

Somehow, miraculously, I survived . . . for the time being. Somehow, in the midst of all this turmoil, God saw me and protected my life. He had a plan for me that would one day be revealed—but not before I would pass through many deep and dark waters.

2

JOURNEY TO KENYA

By the time I was ten, years of civil war had already claimed the lives of many of our Dinka men as they fought to protect their families. This meant boys as young as me— even as young as eight—were trained to take their places within the defense force. In the village where we lived, our chief chose a number of boys to be trained to join the Sudanese People's Liberation Army. Our traditional coming-of-age initiation rituals became proving grounds for combat. Instead of promotion to marriage and leadership, teenage boys headed off to the military.

Having just passed the test of surviving on my own in the bush with my age-mates, I was among the chosen, proud to join the men in defending my people. I knew no other life. War had consumed my childhood and set the parameters of any future I could imagine.

I was preparing for deployment when I began to feel increasingly tired and weak. I had been sick often as a child, but this was an illness like no other. Soon my legs could no longer fully support my weight, and I began to use a stick for walking. I now couldn't join my friends for training to defend my people. They departed, and I was left behind in my village with the women and children.

I was the son of a *beny*, a sort of military officer, and many had high expectations of me. But now I was embarrassed. I felt diminished as a young man—and like a failure and a disappointment to my father. Baba was a leader and defender of his people, and he wanted so much for me to display my own valor. But I could not seem to will my body into strength. Instead, it continued to fail me.

It would be years before I could see God's grace in that moment in my life. Many of my age-mates lost their lives in the civil war, and that very well could have been my fate. But God was saving me for another purpose—again, one I wouldn't realize for some time.

***

As a community, we remained closely bonded. Our survival depended on it, our village no longer a place but its people. We were bound together as a wandering tribe in a common struggle. We were also bonded by a shared Christian faith. It kept us hopeful even as we lamented our suffering. When we set up camp in a new place, we gathered every Sunday, young and old, under a large tree to worship. Led by an elder among us, we would cry out to God for his mercy and peace.

As I grew older, I began to pay more attention to our elder's messages. One Sunday—I was about ten years old—I listened as he opened his tattered Bible and shared, in our language, from John 3:16: "For God so loved the world, that he gave his only Son, that whoever believes in him should not perish but have eternal life." I was deeply moved by the idea of God's love. We had always been a hated people, and it seemed our lives were worth little to the rest of the world.

But the elder spoke of a love that extended to us . . . to me. Many Dinka had reluctantly sent their sons to the frontlines to fight on behalf of the village, but here God had willingly sent his Son—his only Son—to save our lives. Not just our earthly lives but our eternal lives as well. We had so little control over this life, but the elder spoke of a future secure with God in heaven. We were essentially waiting to die. Knowing that Jesus had secured a home for me gave me great hope. I had a ticket to heaven.

That newfound outlook carried me through the many hardships that lay ahead.

***

As my condition worsened, my community prayed for me, but I knew how they secretly saw me. I was half-dead to them—like one waiting in an open grave. To become disabled was to lose one's value. It was to become a burden. The village elder tried to encourage me with the Bible's story of the man who'd been lame for thirty-eight years and then healed by Jesus, and I longed for Christ to see me and offer me the same miracle.

One day, out of the blue, my father made an announcement: "You and I are going to Kakuma Refugee Camp in Kenya to get help for you." We knew some of the Dinka had fled to that camp and that medical assistance was available there. However, the journey would take us at least two months, with a seemingly endless hardship of walking and camping, and always having little to no food or water and facing the danger of encountering wild animals.

I immediately resisted the idea. "No, Baba. I cannot take you away." Not only had I been unable to join in defending my community, but if my father took me to Kenya, I would be taking away my family's protector. My mother would be left alone to care for my four younger siblings, one of whom was just an infant. She had always been a kind and loving mother, willing to give everything for her family. When there was little food, she went hungry so her children could eat. But how would she manage *this* sacrifice?

"How will Mama find enough food for the family on her own? What will happen if the village is attacked?" I asked my father.

But Baba had made up his mind and was determined to go. I was overcome with emotions—fear for what lay ahead and guilt for leaving my mother and siblings with no provider and protector. The thought that I might never see them again was unbearable. Mama, though, had only my welfare on her mind. She had been the rock of the family, a woman who trusted God through the deepest pain and loss a mother's heart could bear. Now she entrusted another son to God's care.

"Go, my son. We want you to have every opportunity possible to get well," she said. "The Lord will protect and provide while you and Baba are away."

What an immense act of love and selflessness.

My father and the leaders of the community mapped out the journey, an impossible trek of almost two hundred miles that would take us two months. We had no money and no means of transportation. But we were desperate, and desperation drives people to do the unthinkable. We would walk, and when I could not walk, my father would carry me on his back.

***

It was the middle of the rainy season when we set out. The Nile had overflowed its banks, and most of the ground we had to walk along was flooded. Our feet often trod on slippery silt and clay. There was no path or road to follow, and we had no navigation equipment. Because we were going south, we tried to use the sun as our compass. We weren't entirely successful, though, and at times we were lost.

We'd travel for miles in search of dry ground where we could set up for the night. Once we found a place, we gathered what dry sticks we could find to build a fire—to ward off both the mosquitoes that tormented us and the roaming wild animals that would not come near a fire. But when it rained and everything was soddened, there could be no fire. There was no reprieve from the elements or insects, and no means of preparing what little food we could find. On those nights, my father kept vigil over me, fanning away the mosquitoes so I could rest.

On the nights when my pain was unbearable and I could not sleep, Baba told me stories of his own life as a boy. There was no war then, and he and the other boys led great herds of cattle across the grasslands to the low plains by the Nile and their water and pasture. Back then, a young man seeking a wife could amass up to two hundred cows as a bride price. The more cows he had, the more wives he could marry and the more children he could have. A man with many children was esteemed in the community.

"One day this fighting will all be over, and your strength will return," my father told me. "You won't need to go to war. You'll have your own herd, son. You'll find a wife and have your own sons and daughters. We just need to get you well."

I tried so hard to walk, but in the end my father carried me most of the way. He would leave me on a dry spot and walk for miles, trying to find dry ground where we could next rest. Then when he found a dry patch, he came back for me.

What with wild animals all around and warring tribes in hiding, it was a dangerous journey for us. I worried that we would not make it. My dad carried a spear and a knife, but these were all we had to defend ourselves. What if something happened to us? I knew my mother was deeply concerned. If we perished along the way, how would the rest of the family even find out we died? Just what would happen to my mother and siblings if we never returned to them?

I came to a point in my thinking when I didn't want Baba to carry me anymore. I just wanted him to leave me to die and go back to the rest of the family. I had completely given up.

Some nights my father became despondent. He, too, was at the brink of losing hope. With surprising candor, he shared his heart with me. He had no wealth. He had few tangible possessions to establish himself as a man. He had lost his first wife in childbirth, and with her their child. Starvation had taken two more young sons, my brothers. With my remaining brother only two years old, and knowing he could die like so many other children had, Baba considered me his sole male heir. Yet my future was uncertain.

At times Baba became bitter with God. Despite his great effort to stand up and defend his community and family, he watched as it all slipped from his grasp. He wondered if my death would be the end of his legacy. To my father, God had taken everything.

This period of our journey was the most time I would ever spend with Baba. Like all the men in the village, his life had been consumed with defending his people. He and other leaders had set up a guard post about an hour's walk from our home to protect us against attacks on the perimeter of our community. He was rarely present to participate in home and community life. He was a rugged, determined man, vigilant and toughened by war and loss.

And now, when I begged him to let us turn back, he encouraged me to be resilient. But I did not know if that was possible. The pain I experienced was unbearable!

After a month of travel, my father and I made it to a small humanitarian camp. There we met a distant uncle of mine who welcomed us to rest with him for a period of time until we started traveling again. The journey had taken a great toll on my body, so I was thankful for respite and food. Some medical workers were at the camp, but they could offer me only pain medication. While I appreciated their attempts to alleviate my suffering, my pain in my back was so severe, my legs were becoming weaker and the medication did nothing to stop my agony. How could I continue the journey?

One evening, a few weeks after we arrived, a humanitarian worker piloting a small plane stopped at the camp for the night. My father and uncle immediately went to request his help to get across the border into Kenya. He said no; it was not allowed. We had heard this before. Other planes had landed and taken off leaving us behind. But we were desperate now, and my uncle, who spoke the pilot's language, pleaded on our behalf.

The pilot's heart softened. He would take us, but he would be leaving promptly at 5 a.m. the next morning with or without us.

We had no clocks, wristwatches, or any other way of knowing the time. Not wanting to risk missing the flight or having the pilot change his mind, Baba and I slept on the tarmac next to the plane. Anticipating the flight and being afraid something would go wrong at the last minute, we were restless the whole night. This was our last hope.

The next morning, the pilot arrived at 4:30 and loaded us on to the plane. Even strapped in and waiting to take off, I was afraid something would prevent us from traveling. But, finally, the plane taxied down the runway, and then we were in the air. Tears of joy and relief streamed down my face. For a boy raised in the bush, this plane ride was an awe-filled experience. I marveled at the sunrise on the horizon and the green countryside spread out below us. It all seemed so peaceful. Flying above, one could hardly imagine the misery and strife on the ground.

The flight to Kenya was more than three hours long. We arrived with no money and no documentation. An official instructed us to continue on to Kakuma Refugee Camp in northern Kenya, a three-hour ride by bus. But we had no funds. We didn't even speak the language to try to negotiate a ride. I watched my father pray for help, and then we waited.

A young man, noticing us just standing around looking confused, asked if we needed help. Someone translated for us, and then he offered to cover our fare. Soon we gestured our great gratitude to him and boarded a small bus for the journey. It was my first experience of traveling on smoothly paved roads. As we rode, I watched Turkana boys my own age herd their cattle near the roadside. The Turkanas were a tribe of pastoralists who made their home in the region. I thought back to the time when we had our own livestock, but now our herds were all gone.

"Look, Baba." I pointed to the Turkana. "They have livestock."

"There is no war here," my father answered, perhaps thinking back to the stories he'd told me about his own youth.

I had no idea what experiencing a place with peace would mean for my future—if anything. As Baba had said, "First we have to get you well." God had provided what I'd needed so far, and I prayed he would continue to do so as my father and I entered this new phase of our journey. Perhaps we would at last know some peace in our souls.

3

KAKUMA

As we traveled to Kakuma Refugee Camp on the bus, the landscape changed from familiar forest land to the arid desert of northwestern Kenya.

Kakuma means "nowhere" in the language of the Turkana, and the camp was unlike any place I had ever been. It had been established to accommodate the thousands of so-called Lost Boys, six- and seven-year-old unaccompanied children fleeing war in Southern Sudan. In 2004, more than 100,000 refugees lived at Kakuma, and today its population has swelled even larger. Refugees from Ethiopia, Somalia, Rwanda, and other neighboring countries lived in makeshift tents, crowded together across the camp as far as the eye could see. A river of displaced people bustled along dusty roads. Children ran freely or gathered in groups to play.

We traveled around the camp in search of our tribesmen, hoping to find someone we knew, perhaps even a relative. Finally, we located some of our people in the Bor section. It was a relief to discover them and communicate freely again in our language. Kakuma, a place of refuge, was also a place of joyful reunion.

We were welcomed as we shared the story of our journey, and then we explained our family history, hoping to find some relatives living in the camp. Those we chatted with knew and reunited us with my father's cousin, who was quick to share her food and possessions. We also found my mother's younger brother, Abraham. We'd been sure he had been killed. Those raids on our village had separated many families, and we'd had no way of knowing who had survived and who had died.

My father and I cried when we were reunited with Abraham . . . and he cried at my sad state.

A young man in his early twenties, Abraham was humble and caring and full of joy despite our situation. He became our chief sponsor as we adjusted to our new life. Less than a decade older, he quickly became my friend and role model. Later, he played an essential role in my journey to recovery.

Early in the morning the day after our arrival, Abraham took us to the camp clinic for me to be evaluated. Even at such an early hour, the lines were long with people plagued with various ailments. Though I was in pain and had to wait my turn, I was grateful for this very first opportunity to receive answers and treatment.

But the clinic had little equipment, and only a few staff members attempted to serve thousands. The clinic also had no ability to do X-rays or blood tests. It was a terrible letdown when they told us they could not diagnose or truly address my illness. Once again, we were sent on our way with only pain medication. All the days of walking and being carried had been for nothing. All the nights of sleeping on the ground had been wasted. It had all been a long, difficult journey to disappointment.

***

Months passed at Kakuma, and my pain and paralysis grew progressively worse. I could do little for myself. My father carried me everywhere, even to bathe and use the public latrine. I grew increasingly depressed and frustrated. What would become of me? What use was there for my life? It seemed to me that it would be better for me to die than to live in this condition. I cried out to God: *Where are you? Why have you brought us all this way for nothing?*

Even though Kakuma is a refugee camp, some of the children were being trained in schools set up there. But none of the schools were equipped to handle the mobility issues of a young person in my condition. Perhaps I could be trained in a trade? But that, too, was impossible for me. So great was my pain that I could barely concentrate on any kind of learning.

Each morning, I sat at the doorway of our tent and watched as children passed by on their way to school. I had a great hunger for knowledge, and I longed for an opportunity to be educated. Back in my village, my people had recognized my potential. They called me *akiim*, "doctor." When we were living in a more stable location, I had traveled a four-hour round trip with some of the boys of my village to be taught by a man from a neighboring clan. We had no books and no paper to even write on. Instead, gathered under a tree, we used sticks to copy our teacher's strokes, scratching out the alphabet in the dirt. A deep desire for learning grew in me, and it never faded.

Here in Kakuma Refugee Camp, schooling was almost in sight, yet just out of my reach.

Peering out from the darkness of our tent at the goings-on of our corner of the camp, I watched young boys play ball after school and remembered the days when I, too, could run and kick with ease.

In the evenings, my father carried me out under the stars. With no lights from a city, the stars were very bright—and there were so many of them. Looking up into the peaceful night sky always comforted me. I felt as though I was gazing into the face of God himself.

I recalled that elder in our village teaching us about heaven—the place with no sorrow, no pain, no suffering. My whole being longed for such relief. Perhaps, out there under the stars, God would see my face from above and rescue me from my despair. Or maybe he would take me to live with him. To me, my life on earth had become a living hell.

One evening, Uncle Abraham visited us with great news. He had heard that a team of medical missionaries would be arriving in a few weeks to offer a clinical outreach in our camp. They were from CURE Hospital in

Kijabe, and they were coming to see children with physical deformities such as clubfoot and spina bifida. These were conditions that could be easily treated with surgeries and the right medical care, but medical care was lacking in Kakuma. Many children in our camp suffered from these fixable deformities.

My situation, however, was a little different. Whatever was ailing me had left my spine contorted. I wondered if anything could be done for me at this point. It had been more than a year since my symptoms first emerged, and I had grown steadily worse, day by day and month by month.

I prayed, counting the days until these angels from CURE Hospital were due to arrive. I could hardly sleep the night before the clinic. By dawn, my father and I had joined the horde of people standing outside the clinic area seeking help. Many had spent the night camped in a queue. Like me, they had waited for months in pain and with little hope. For many of us, this clinic seemed our last chance.

It took only a brief exam for the doctors to diagnose my illness—tuberculosis of the spine. They had seen it before, and I would need surgery as soon as possible. They requested that I be transferred to the CURE Hospital in Kijabe, which was best outfitted to treat me. CURE Hospital is a missionary medical facility offering orthopedic surgeries and rehabilitative care to youth. Their services are free to families who cannot afford their children's medical expenses. But the hospital was small— only thirty beds—and the waiting list to be admitted was long. I would have to wait another six months in Kakuma before I could go to Kijabe.

Waiting seemed to be every person's chief occupation here, and those six months felt like six years. Our hard life continued in the camp. We were free of war, but a poor diet of rationed food caused my health to deteriorate even further and faster. Frequent flooding brought cholera to the camp. Sandstorms chafed our skin and irritated our lungs. Meanwhile, I sat quietly in the doorway of our tent, biding my time, imagining myself whole again and able to participate in all that passed me by.

Would that day ever come?

4

HOPE DEFERRED

"Wake up, Michael. It's time for you to go to the CURE Hospital," my father said as he shook me awake. The UN had arranged and sponsored my trip to Kijabe from Kakuma, and I would travel by bus. But we were shocked to learn I would be going alone. The UN would pay only my fare, and since we had no funds of our own to pay for Baba or another relative to travel with me, I would have to go by myself.

"Michael, can you do this on your own?" my father asked. "Can you manage?" For over a year, he and I had been inseparable, traveling across Sudan and Kenya together, then living in the refugee camp. When I became too weak to walk, he had been the one to carry me wherever I needed to go. I had grown close to him, and now we would part ways for who knew how long. It was a difficult goodbye.

I was concerned not only for those I left behind at Kakuma but for my mother and siblings back in Sudan. We had been gone from them far longer than I ever imagined we would, and we had no way to know how they fared.

Nor would my father be returning to them, as he would be waiting for me in Kakuma. Now, in saying goodbye to my father, I was letting go of my last connection to family and tribe. Would we ever be reunited?

So little in my life was guaranteed.

Baba and Uncle Abraham carried me to the station and helped me to my seat on the bus. Sitting around me were other wide-eyed and anxious youth, their bodies as bent and painful as my own. We left late in the afternoon on what turned out to be a seventeen-hour journey. I waved goodbye as long as I could see Baba and Uncle Abraham.

I wondered if and how I could survive on my own. Would I truly be healed? Could I be?

The bus driver steered on and on through a stormy night. Paved highways turned to deeply rutted roads, and each bump bounced us around in our seats as heavy rain pounded the metal roof of the bus. With no lower-body control, I had to hold on tightly to keep from falling out of my seat. I slept in snatches. Outside, flashes of lightning lit up the night sky. My mind played and replayed the fact that I had left my family behind me, first Mama and my siblings, and now my father and everyone I knew at Kakuma Refugee Camp. I had no idea what lay ahead for this eleven-year-old boy.

When we stopped twice to change tires and for inspection of our documents, everyone else got off the bus to use the restroom. But I couldn't walk, and I didn't want strangers to help me. I also worried that the bus might leave me and I would be stranded. I was very uncomfortable.

As day dawned, I awoke to a surprising scene. The dry, barren conditions of the Northern Rift Valley had faded away and been replaced by the lush greenery and rich earth of the central highlands of Kenya. A cool breeze was a refreshing change from harsh, sandy camp winds. From outside the bus, I heard birds just as I once had in the forests of my homeland.

We had seemingly gone on a journey from *nowhere* to *life*. My heart lifted, and I was filled with anticipation.

***

After a day and a half on the bus, we arrived at our destination. I was tired, soaked in my own urine, and so grateful to finally be off the bus and at CURE Hospital. A pleasant staff member helped me into a wheelchair and wheeled me to the nurses.

"Where is your guardian?" a translator asked.

"I am alone," I said.

My heart sank as I learned they could not perform the operation on me without an adult present. At age eleven I was too young to consent. "We will need to send a message back to Kakuma for someone to come and represent you."

Once again, the surgery would have to wait.

A nurse assigned me to my bed, then wheeled me toward the bay of showers so I could take the first shower of my life. The warm water beat against my skin, soothing my sore muscles and washing urine, months of travel, and Kakuma dirt from my body.

My first days at CURE were filled with new experiences—wonderful experiences. I drank my first warm cup of chai tea and ate delicious *mandazi*, a kind of donut, for breakfast. But that was just the beginning of my amazement: there followed the wheelchair, the flushing toilet, the light fixture above my bed, a soft pillow, and a clean mattress. At least for now, I had left behind life on a mat on the dirty floor of our crudely constructed tent. Gone were the heat, the noise, the mosquitoes, and the poor food.

I slept well that first night. Then the next day, American missionary physician Dr. Tim Mead and his Kenyan partner, Dr. Joseph Theuri, arrived to examine me. I remembered Dr. Theuri as the physician who had examined me in Kakuma Refugee Camp and approved my transfer to CURE. The doctors were gentle and kind. Together, they confirmed my condition as tuberculosis of the spine with paralysis from the chest down. I had likely contracted the disease from drinking raw milk, and it had done enough damage to threaten my life. Had I not been so malnourished when my body was first exposed, I could have fought off the infection. And if I had been treated with antibiotics early enough, I would have recovered fully.

But now perhaps it was too late to expect such an outcome. War greatly limits people's access to health care. It creates waves of death and devastation. Where bullets and machetes do not take life, disease and famine do their work.

As I waited my turn for surgery, my mind ran wild. *How large will the knife be? Will I be in pain? How long will it take for me to heal?* My young mind had not yet come to terms with the reality that I would never be the same as I once was. I imagined my body fully healed. I saw myself walking out of the hospital restored to full function.

Uncle Abraham could not join me until he had completed his high school exams, and my father did not know the language here in Kijabe. So Nathaniel, a member of my tribe living at Kakuma, came to represent me so the surgery could be done. A week later, Dr. Mead and Dr. Theuri prepared to perform the surgery. They wanted to decompress my spinal cord and stabilize my spine. It was a risky operation, but there was no alternative.

Early on the morning of the surgery, my nurses came in to see me. "Good morning, Michael. This is an important day for you. We have to get you ready for surgery, and that means a bath." When they had finished, other nurses and the doctors came in to pray with me and to encourage me before the procedure.

"Are you ready to go?" someone asked.

Ready to go? I wasn't sure, but what other option did I have? I nodded, and they began wheeling me down the hallway. While I was so nervous lying there in the operating room, I was comforted knowing men and women of faith surrounded me. The nurses and anesthesiologist tried to calm my nerves. Soon the doctors arrived, and I could hear them discussing how they would tackle the surgery. Beside me, a nurse took my arm, searched for a vein, and injected the anesthesia. I drifted off to sleep.

I woke up late that evening back in my room. The surgery had taken eight hours. A nurse was there checking my vital signs, and an oxygen mask was over my face. The pain was excruciating, and I struggled through that first, long night.

"Michael, how are you feeling?" the doctors asked when they visited me the following morning.

Did they want me to tell the truth? I felt terrible.

"Can you wiggle your toes?" one of them asked. I could, and the doctors seemed satisfied with my progress.

That day, I drifted in and out of sleep with little awareness of what was going on around me. But over the next few days, my hopes were dashed as complications arose. I felt weak. I struggled for breath. I could hear the monitors beeping as I drifted in and out of consciousness.

"His oxygen levels are very low," my doctors said. Suddenly, I was rushed out of CURE Hospital and to the ICU of the local general hospital, where I was placed on a ventilator. I was miserable, and I was *terrified*. The following morning, the doctors awakened me to remove the breathing tube. As soon as they did, though, we realized I could no longer breathe on my own. I needed a tracheostomy.

Unlike CURE, this facility was big and busy. I could hear the groaning of patients in pain. Others were aggressively crying out for assistance. These were very sick people in critical condition, and so was I. As I lay there on my back for twenty-one days, I was unable to speak or even eat. Once again, I wondered if I would survive. Uncle Abraham, who by now had replaced Nathaniel as my adult in charge, was by my side. He comforted me the best he could.

Slowly, so slowly, my lungs improved. At last, though still with a breathing tube, I was able to return to CURE. Everyone feared it could never be removed if I were to live. My doctors, however, were able to withdraw my feeding tube, and I was grateful to be able to eat again.

In this state, though, I had little joy and little confidence that anything would ever change. At best, I seemed to be merely existing. This was so far from the outcome I had imagined for myself. Weeks passed as I lay flat on my back, unable to speak or breathe on my own. I watched new roommates come and go while I waited for specialists to come from the United States to assess my condition. I was sure I would die before they arrived.

I had been low before, but this was my lowest point. I had hit rock bottom emotionally and physically.

Then, one day, a young man named Earnest joined the staff as the hospital chaplain. Earnest was passionate about the Lord and his own role as a messenger of good news to his young patients.

"Good morning, Michael," he said as he came into my room each morning. I was always his first visit. With his Bible in hand, he sat at my bedside and read portions of Scripture to Abraham and me. I understood little of what he was saying in those early months because we did not speak the same language, but I welcomed his visits anyway. His kind face and smile, and the sincerity of his expression as he prayed, gave me courage and calmed my anxieties about my condition.

Finally, the specialists arrived. After their exam, they agreed to perform another surgery. I headed into the operating room sure I would now be free of the breathing tube. But hours later, I awakened to feel the familiar pressure against my throat. I was still unable to breathe on my own or speak. I touched the tubing, motioning to Abraham: *What happened?* The ear, nose, and throat doctors' assessment had not been good, and they had refused to do the surgery.

"Michael, I'm so sorry. They had to leave the tube in place. It was too risky to remove it," Abraham told me. Once again, my hopes were dashed.

To make matters worse, since there was nothing more they could do for me, CURE wanted to discharge me from its care. I was terrified. No one at Kakuma Refugee Camp was equipped to provide the level of care I needed. Abraham begged to see Dr. Mead and Dr. Theuri. They were deeply concerned and nodded in agreement.

"If we send him back to Kakuma in this condition," they said, "he'll never get better. He'll die from infection."

Dr. Mead and Dr. Theuri prayed and fasted for wisdom for a month, and they refused to give up on me. I was the first patient they evaluated every morning, and they worked hard to find a life-saving solution. One day, they proposed that they attempt the same surgery the specialists had refused. It would be risky as they were not trained to perform this particular procedure, but they were willing to do it.

"Michael, you understand the risk," one of them said. "What would you like us to do?"

"Operate. I have nothing to lose at this point." I trusted these men and put my life in their hands. The Lord had gifted them with great skill. They were also men of true faith who were humbly relying on God.

On the day of the surgery, the CURE team gathered once again around my bed to pray for me and for the doctors. The surgery took more than ten hours. I awoke late that night very groggy but grateful to be alive. And wonder of wonders, I could breathe on my own! I cleared my throat and could hear my raspy voice for the first time in three months. My nurse praised God.

"*Asante*," I said, speaking my first words in Swahili. *Thank you*. Filled with gratitude, I started to praise the Lord and thank everyone, whether or not they were in the room. My nurse urged me to protect my voice, but in my excitement, I could not keep quiet. She administered a sedative, and once again, I drifted off to sleep.

Recovery was not easy. My trachea continued to threaten collapse. For four months, I endured repeated dilatations to ensure I could breathe. At one point, the doctors feared they would need to reinsert the breathing tube. But overall their procedure was a success, and eventually, I was breathing well on my own. To me, it was a miracle. I had started my journey to recovery.

I remained in the hospital several more weeks to be observed and receive therapy. I learned to use a walker, then crutches. My left leg was weak, but the right one was gaining strength daily. I was determined to walk. One of the chaplains arranged for me to be discharged to spend time with his sons. It was an opportunity to develop friendships and improve my English and Swahili.

All seemed to be going well until around the beginning of the new year—about a year and a half after I first arrived at CURE. Once again, I felt a familiar weakness in my legs.

My doctors examined me. "Michael, we hate to have to tell you this, but your spine is compressed again," they said. My heart sank to my toes. The doctors and staff were discouraged, and I was afraid. No one wanted me to have to go through surgery again—not with the complications I had faced. But there was no choice. "If we don't operate, your whole body will become fully paralyzed," they told me.

I was sure this would now be my end.

Dr. Mead performed the surgery. But as he and the other doctors had feared, this life-saving procedure ended any chance that I would recover the use of my legs. I awoke from surgery to find I had no feeling in them. My hopes were dashed one more time. I would never walk again. My world had been turned upside down. I could never be the person I was before. I struggled to accept that reality.

This time my father traveled from Kakuma Refugee Camp to be with me for the surgery. I knew enough Swahili so that I no longer needed Abraham's help to translate. It had been months since I had seen my father, who had waited alone in the camp at Kakuma with little word of my condition. This was not the way I wanted our reunion to be. Not what I had hoped for. I had been through many procedures and months of rehabilitation only to find myself in a similar physical state as when I arrived.

The days passed, Baba in a chair by my bed, distressed about my state and anxious about my mother and siblings back in Sudan. It had been over two years since we'd had any contact with them.

"Baba, please go home to the family," I finally said. We could not let them die while we waited for a healing, especially when my life was in such jeopardy. "You can go. I'll be all right. These are wonderful people, and they will care for me."

It was agreed that if there were complications, my CURE family would send for Abraham. And so, reluctantly, my father left me and returned to the old village. I would be a grown man before I laid eyes on him again.

***

I spent almost two years in CURE Hospital—longer than any other patient. I became a child of the place, raised by the doctors and their wives, the nurses, and the support staff. They embraced me as their own, and when I was strong enough, I was eager to learn from them. Each day, I tried to learn five words in Swahili.

I also learned to wheel myself up and down the hospital corridors in one of three wheelchairs. As I was weak and recuperating, and the chairs simply swallowed up my small frame, at first it was difficult and frustrating to maneuver them. But I liked one chair better than the others, so every morning, I claimed it. When the nurses couldn't find the chair, they knew I probably had it. They soon gave up and called it "Michael's chair."

The chair was still too big for me, but its big wheels on the front would go over the grass better than the others. I remember the first day I wheeled out into the sunshine and fresh air to catch a glimpse of Mount Longonot rising up from the Rift Valley floor. It was wonderful to be outdoors!

When I had setbacks in my health, though, hopelessness would creep up on me. I wrestled with God: *Why is this happening to me? Why can't I get better? I hate my life!* In my culture, permanently disabled people have no place in society, so I could not even return home.

***

God brought many mentors into my life who shared their own faith stories and pointed me to the Lord. Slowly, I began to break free from a mindset of being useless and without hope. These key people helped me see my situation in light of God's goodness and plan.

Why had I survived being lost at such a young age? When our village was attacked, I could easily have died from exposure or at the hands of attacking forces. How had I survived a one-month-long trek through flooded ground when I could not walk? Why, after others said no, had that pilot agreed to fly us to Kenya, where perhaps I could find help? I stopped to consider not only all this but more of what I had been through. Those last months in the hospital became the most important period of discipleship in my life.

As I recovered and my Swahili improved, Earnest shared more of the good news of the gospel. He spoke with humility as he walked me through the book of Romans. He taught me about my sin and the holiness and judgment of God. He told me about God's mercy and salvation in Christ. I had never heard a full gospel presentation before, only the bits and pieces the elder had shared. Earnest read to me from the book of Philippians, and I learned of Paul declaring, "For to me to live is Christ, and to die is gain" (Philippians 1:21). That was new to my thinking about what it meant to be a Christian. I had many questions, and Earnest patiently answered them.

Even as I wrestled with my own disappointment at not being healed, I wanted to trust in the goodness and sovereignty of the Lord. But I was not there yet.

Francesca was a member of the patient care team offering social and spiritual support. If the nurses were like mothers to me, Francesca was like a big sister. I always looked forward to her visits. She shone as light at a very dark time in my life. She, too, was disabled. As a teenager, she had lost her leg to disease. She became a symbol of hope to me—my first glimpse of a full life with a disability. If she could thrive, maybe I could too. When at my lowest, when I was sure I could not take much more, Francesca came to my bedside to comfort me. She played an important part in my recovery, not only physically but spiritually.

One day, she said, "Michael, some of the other children and I are going to the playroom to see a movie. Would you like to come?"

"Yes," I said. "I would like to get out of this room."

I had only a little grasp of English at the time, so I didn't fully understand what the movie was about. I mainly watched the images moving on the screen and tried to understand the story. The movie showed a teenager who suffered a diving accident and, like me, became paralyzed. Later, I learned the movie was the story of Joni Eareckson Tada. She, too, had spent months in hospital in pain. She, too, had to come to terms with her loss and her new reality. This was all familiar to me. I understood.

In the movie, I saw others encouraging her to read her Bible. As she did, joy slowly returned to her face. Francesca explained the parts I didn't understand. She said, "The Lord had a plan for Joni's life. Instead of the accident ending her life, it became a way for her to reach millions of people with a message of hope in Christ."

As Francesca talked, a little thought wormed its way into my mind: *Could it be that the Lord intended to use me even in my wheelchair?* Yet I could not begin to imagine what he might have in store for me.

Francesca was such an important part of my life that when she was to be married, she invited me to join the celebration. I was discharged for a few hours so I could attend her wedding and act as a groomsman. It was the first time I had ever worn a suit or had my picture taken. I did not know I should smile for the camera, but a heart full of joy was inside of me. I could almost see a vision of hope for a full and meaningful life, even though I had a disability. This was a vision full of life, love, and acceptance.

In the hospital, the nurses had more time to spend with me at night. I would stay awake to have long talks with them and practice both my English and Swahili. They loved me and cared deeply about my well-being.

Among them was Miriam. In her childhood, she had been badly burned on her face and hand. She shared with me how this left her feeling self-conscious and ashamed. So often in our native cultures, any deformity could cause open derision from others. She told me that people stared at and rejected her. But Miriam was a believer in Jesus. She knew God, and she learned to see herself as God saw her. She urged me to begin to find my own identity in Christ. Miriam was one of the most joyful people I would meet and befriend at CURE Hospital. I came to realize that the source of her joy was her relationship with Jesus Christ.

In the months I spent recovering at CURE, I had many questions for God, the chief of which was: *Do you truly love me?* With Earnest's help, I came to understand the Bible, but some questions persisted. Corinne, the wife of one of the missionary doctors, gave me my first Bible in English and Swahili. Stories like that of the man born blind became my story. In them, I saw the love of God extended toward people with disabilities. Jesus didn't deride them; he saw them, touched them, and healed them.

I learned that Jesus used the experiences of those he healed to display his glory. The Lord began to impress on my heart that my disability was not happenstance. He was at work. He had purpose in what I was facing! It was a long-fought journey, but I began to trust the Lord and develop a new perspective. Looking back, I saw that he was in fact saving my life through this illness. I recognized the hand of God on me.

Slowly, ever so slowly, joy replaced despair. Finally, I found peace.

The CURE Hospital became my home. As my English and Swahili improved and I grew in my relationship with the Lord, I roamed the halls of the facility as an ambassador of hope, encouraging young, fellow patients. I met Ann, a young girl with a spinal issue like mine. When she arrived, she was covered with bedsores from being confined to her bed. She was in pain and low in spirits. I took her on as my first assignment. She was, as I had been, a nominal Christian. Wavering in her faith, she was full of the same questions with which I had wrestled. To cheer her up, I would pull out all that had been shared with me over the past months to encourage me and correct my thinking. In the process of teaching her, I anchored my own heart in truth.

Ramathani arrived at CURE Hospital with his father to have his clubfoot corrected. He was an older teenager, and he was Muslim. His case was complicated by his age and the time he had spent without treatment. His surgeries and recovery required a longer stay at CURE than the average patient. This gave us an opportunity to get to know each other well. I was happy to gain a friend who was closer to my age. Ramathani and I spent our days together in a corner of the hospital's recreation room, away from the noise of the younger children.

One day, he sank into the narrow pediatric furniture and propped up his healing leg as best he could. He was bored. "Do you want to read this?" I offered in broken Swahili. I handed him a book in simple English. To improve my English and help me grow in my faith, Corinne had given me children's books of Bible stories to read.

"I don't read English. What does it say?" Ramathani asked.

"Jesus loves me. *Yesu Kristo*."

"I'm not interested," he told me.

I had guessed from his father's dress that they were Muslim. Religion had been an undercurrent of the war between Sudan and South Sudan. The Islamic government of the North had fueled and funded intertribal conflict in the South. Muslims had caused our tribe to flee repeatedly from vicious attacks. At Kakuma, however, I had seen people of various faiths coexisting, keeping largely to their own sections of the camp in a mutual struggle for survival.

At CURE, I had found myself surrounded by Christians, and everyone spoke freely of Jesus. Ramathani posed a new challenge for me. I was eager to share with him about the Lord, but I worried my cheerful evangelism would prove more of an offense than an invitation to him.

Adjusting my approach, I asked, "Do you want to hear what I have been learning about Jesus?" That week, Earnest had shared with me from Matthew 11:28–30: "Come to me, all who labor and are heavy laden, and I will give you rest. Take my yoke upon you, and learn from me, for I am gentle and lowly in heart, and you will find rest for your souls. For my yoke is easy, and my burden is light."

I still wrestled with weariness over my paralysis and the slow progress I was making, but Earnest had showed me how Jesus offered an invitation to rest in him. I knew Ramathani was restless with his condition. Like me, his disability had limited his prospects and had shaped society's perception of him. His was a birth defect, so he had carried the stigma of his condition his whole life. It would take more than surgery to reform his identity.

I was happy that Ramathani was open to sharing back and forth about our faiths. We even sparred at times on the topic. Perhaps he humored me at first because there was little else to do during those hours in the playroom. But in time, I could tell I had piqued his interest. I told him of man's sin—how all humans have rebelled against God and deserve his punishment. But so great is God's love for people that it caused him to give his own Son on behalf of sinners. Mohammed had made no such offer. There was no mediator in his Islam faith, no good news of penalties paid. Sharing the little bit of discipleship and learning I had received from Earnest and Francesca, and in my limited Swahili, I witnessed to my friend. I then watched as the Holy Spirit took my feeble efforts and moved Ramathani's heart.

"How do you know these things?" he would ask, and I would tell him of my time with Earnest each morning and the difference it was making in my outlook. I gave him my copy of the Bible in Swahili. He read it but out of sight of his father. Francesca was always with us in the playroom, and she found books for Ramathani in Swahili that were more appropriate for his age. She also answered his deeper questions.

In time, Ramathani's father's heart softened—how could it not? For months, he had watched Christian doctors and nurses offer his son a new life through surgeries and therapies. He had observed their tenderness and compassion and the love given in Jesus's name. He may not have sanctioned his son's exploration of Christianity, but he did not prevent it.

Toward the end of his stay, Ramathani prayed with Corinne to receive Christ. There is no way of knowing how he negotiated his new faith once he left the safe and free environment of CURE and returned to his community, but he departed with the seed of truth planted firmly in good soil.

***

My doctors invested heavily in me, not only as my physicians but increasingly in parenting roles. Two of the people who acted, and have continued to act, as Christ's hands and feet in my life are orthopedic surgeon Dr. Tim Mead and his wife, Jana. To me, they are *Daktari* and Mama Jana. Jana took a particular interest in me, visiting me often to talk in broken Swahili and to bring me books and treats. She even introduced me to my favorite drink, Fanta Orange. The day she met me, Mama Jana handed me a quilt she had made, which I treasure to this day. Mama Jana also prayed with me and joined others in encouraging me to trust the Lord.

In the next chapter, the Meads tell their own story of how they got to Africa at exactly the right time to help me. Their story, too, is an amazing display of God's grace.

5

DR. TIM AND JANA MEAD TELL THEIR STORY

DR. TIM

In 1995, I traveled to Ecuador on a medical mission trip. There I assisted in general surgery rather than in my specialty of orthopedic surgery. The cases were interesting and challenging, but I didn't feel called to mission work. That was despite the local missionary, Baxter Swenson, telling me he knew I would serve overseas someday. I said he was nuts; I was quite happy in private practice. Jana, my wife, was relieved; she didn't feel called to leave our home along the shores of Lake Michigan either!

I knew, however, that before I rejected Swenson's challenge outright, I probably needed to pray about it. So I did. I told God he would have to find a place for me to use my orthopedic surgical skills if I was going to serve as a missionary. Anything else didn't make sense. God, obviously, took me up on that. A couple of months after my return from Ecuador, Jana and I met Dick Bransford, a missionary from Kijabe, Kenya. He told us, "What we really need is an orthopedic surgeon."

And our friend Dick Kamps, who had been to Kijabe as a medical student, told Jana, "I can see you and Tim living there."

In 1997, Jana, our four children, and I traveled to Kijabe for what was to be a *one-time-only*, six-week mission trip. Although I wasn't a "certified" pediatric orthopedic surgeon, many of the patients who awaited care there were children. I stayed busy serving them, and I thought this six-week time of service surely fulfilled God's call for our work overseas.

While in Kijabe, we got to know another orthopedic surgeon there, Dr. Scott Harrison, and his wife, Sally. Scott told me about his dream of a network of hospitals caring for physically disabled children in the developing world. The first hospital, CURE Hospital, was at that moment being built right there in Kijabe. The ground breaking had already taken place, and Scott took me on a "vision walk."

I saw only a few stone blocks and flattened ground, yet he "showed" me the hospital. He pointed to where the wards would be and where the ORs (operating rooms) would be. Then he said this network of hospitals would intentionally provide both spiritual and medical ministry to children—children with little or no hope. The staff would show them the hope and love of Christ.

JANA

When we were told an orthopedic surgeon was needed in Kijabe, I started wondering what I would do if God was really calling us overseas. The truth was I *wasn't* ready. I struggled with panic and anxiety attacks, I hated to fly, and I was afraid of bugs, AIDS, and the unknown.

I decided I needed to get some professional help just in case God *was* calling us to Africa. I went to a counselor to talk through my fears, and I also took medication to help with the panic and anxiety attacks. By the time we left for that first trip to Kijabe with our kids, I thought I could cope. I expected that, after surviving these six weeks, that would be the end of this particular call and challenge from God. I told our church, "It's a miracle that I'm going at all!"

One day in Kijabe, I wanted to do something more than simply care for my family. Something worthwhile. I tried going on a clinic visit, but once I was in the vehicle, I had a panic attack and couldn't set off. I later confided in a friend, Sally Harrison. She told me, "Your job of taking care of your kids is just as important to God as Tim's operating on these kids with disabilities. Tim wouldn't be here without you." I will be forever grateful to God for speaking to my heart through my friend Sally, who calmed my anxiety and fear.

At the time, I didn't know this trip would simply lay the groundwork for God's ultimate plan for us—moving to Kijabe—nor that Michael was one more kid I would someday care for.

DR. TIM

CURE is indeed an intentionally blended medical and spiritual ministry, treating the whole, physically disabled child as well as serving that child's family. It was also instrumental in forming the first certified orthopedic residency program in Kenya.

Many children who came to us presented with complex deformities that are rarely if ever seen in private practice settings or even in university clinics in the United States. Congenital deformities of the hands, lower limbs, and spine are normally referred to specialized medical facilities in Western countries. At the clinic we frequently saw advanced bone infections that defy an easy answer, children who had been burned in open fires with severe scarring, and those with loss of limb function simply because these young patients lacked previous medical care.

Michael was at first called by his surname, Panther or as they pronounced it "Pantha," when he arrived at CURE from Kakuma Refugee Camp. He was a paralyzed young boy with a massive tuberculosis infection eating away the spinal elements of his upper thoracic spine, causing his spine to collapse. We later learned he also had a stenosis of his trachea—a narrowing of his windpipe—from the TB. And besides his physical pain, Michael was dealing with paraplegia, loss of independence, refugee status, starvation, and family separation. He needed all the care CURE could provide.

When we examined Michael, we discovered a sharp angulation of his spine at his chest level. You could probably have balanced a coffee cup on his spine and not spilled a drop. Tuberculosis is a slow-growing infection commonly thought to be only in the lungs, but about 10 percent of people infected with TB have extra-pulmonary infective sites—located outside the lungs. Of those, about half will involve the spine. Michael's spine had more than five destroyed vertebral segments, and there was a bulging abscess in his chest. Left untreated, his paralysis would continue to ascend until he would be unable to breathe. Without treatment, death was certain for him.

Prayer always played a huge role as we treated these children. We needed it. Remember, I was an orthopedic surgeon in private practice in my prior life. Before moving to Kenya, I had never seen a patient with spinal tuberculosis. I had training in surgery of the spine during my residency, but not until I served in Kenya did God provide a teacher for anterior spine surgery—where the spine is approached through the abdomen instead of through the lower back. God had prepared me and the CURE staff for Michael's arrival before he ever arrived.

The risks of surgery were explained to Michael and the family with him. Long travel, poor nutrition, and chronic illness had all taken their toll. The surgical spinal level near the top of his chest was difficult to reach, and the deformity was huge. Following surgery, we would have to continue a multi-drug regimen for the chemical treatment of the tuberculosis for a minimum of six months.

The alternative to this treatment was eventual death. Without expressing any doubt, Michael wanted the operation!

In the recovery room after surgery, Michael's breathing tube was removed, and he started breathing on his own. The chest tube was placed on suction to reinflate the lung and his oxygen levels were augmented through a nasal breathing tube. His vital signs were stable, and his blood counts were reasonable. We were elated but wary at the same time. This was such a serious surgery. The next day when I checked Michael during early rounds, he looked to be doing well. No major changes in care were needed. A few hours later, however, he went into respiratory distress, and the breathing tube had to be replaced into his lungs.

Over the next few days, Michael would do well when the tube was removed, but then he'd slowly return to respiratory distress and the tube would have to go back in. Finally, it was clear that Michael's trachea—the big breathing airway—had an issue from his tuberculosis infection. A surgery on Michael's neck placed a tube, called a tracheostomy, lower in the trachea. But Michael could never return home with this tube in place, so we needed to figure out how to fix his trachea issue.

Eventually, a visiting ENT (ears, nose, and throat) surgical team came, bringing with them a bronchoscope—a telescope-like instrument that can look into the lungs and airways. Looking down Michael's trachea, they discovered a constricted narrowing with the channel of the trachea. That meant any swelling of the trachea would shut off airflow.

Options for treatment in Kenya were limited, and the situation was complicated by the fact Michael suffered respiratory infections. We did what we could without knowing how we could ultimately resolve this issue. Many times I wondered if Michael would survive. And although we continued anti-tuberculosis medication, surgery on the posterior spine was canceled because the risks were just too great.

As time passed, we witnessed a miracle from God: Michael regained some sensation in, and was able to move, his lower limbs. Therapy finally allowed him to walk short distances with crutches. Then, after some medication from another ENT team failed, a "trachea specialist" presented another option: surgery to remove the narrowed section of the trachea approaching the narrowed trachea. Hopefully, the two ends of the trachea could be connected into a single, normal-sized tube.

When a third ENT team refused to do this surgery, which no one had even seen let alone done, I pointed out that the only other option was for a crazy orthopedic surgeon and his partner to perform the case. Amazingly, the ENT team agreed. So Dr. Joseph Theuri—my Kenyan partner, who had earlier trained with me—and I read what we could about trachea surgery, reviewed the relevant anatomy, and most of all prayed for God's grace to intervene in Michael's life. We shared with Michael the two options of living with a tracheostomy or attempting the surgery. He didn't like nor want the tracheostomy tube, so we scheduled the surgery.

CURE team members gathered to pray for Michael, and a surgical plan was formulated. When surgery day arrived, the whole CURE staff gathered at Michael's bedside. At CURE hospitals, the staff prays with and for patients before each surgery. These prayers for Michael were especially fervent as we sought God's grace and protection for him and the whole CURE team.

The surgery progressed, with my stress level spiking when the trachea was cut. Removing the rigid, damaged tracheal section left the two ends we expected, but they might as well have been a mile apart. Plus, the lining couldn't be damaged or all would fail. Nor could we narrow the channel of the trachea; it had to be airtight and not leak. As we say in Kiswahili (another term for Swahili), *Hakuna shida!* No problem. Right?

When we finished, a breathing tube was inserted into his repaired trachea. The tracheostomy tube was removed, and the wound was cleaned and closed. Dr. Theuri and I took a brief time out for a prayer of thanks. In the recovery room, we watched Michael and his breathing tube all night. Many prayers and many cups of chai later, the sun rose, and Michael lived to see another day.

Eventually, we removed the breathing tube, and Michael breathed on his own. Weeks passed, and we became confident as physical therapists continued to mobilize and strengthen his lower extremities. All was going well . . . until disaster struck again with transverse myelitis, an inflammation that interrupts the messages the spinal cord sends to the rest of the body.

Michael's paralysis returned, and no surgery would change that—ever. He would be confined to a wheelchair for the rest of his life. His future was more unknown than ever.

JANA

Michael showed great patience during his waiting times and used them wisely. The only schooling he'd ever had was under a tree in Sudan. However, he was a sharp young man. He had learned Kiswahili and English, and visitors had worked with him on reading and other educational tasks. As Michael says in an earlier chapter, he also grew spiritually, with the help of several others, while recovering from his physical ordeals.

Once Michael no longer had the use of his legs, the staff at CURE struggled with how to help him move forward in life. He couldn't return to Sudan in his condition; he'd have no future there. All the ideas proposed for him were soon discarded as unworkable.

Then God intervened.

Michael and I talked on the phone occasionally, but I didn't visit him at the hospital very often. Then one day in the autumn of 2007, I just came to say hello. I had no agenda in mind; I wasn't thinking about Michael's future.

As we were talking in his private room, I felt like God was standing at my right shoulder. He said to me, "Jana, I want you to take care of Michael."

I replied, "Lord, I already have four kids. I don't need another one."

He again said, "Jana, I want you to take care of Michael." When I looked at Michael, he was still talking to me, but I wasn't listening. My mind was going over what had just happened. What was I to do?

I finished my conversation and went home to find Tim. I told him what God had said to me. Tim knew this was not my idea. He knew it was the voice of God speaking to me. So we didn't pray about it; we just obeyed.

The next day, we told Michael we were giving him a permanent home with our family. That decision was a blessing that continues to this day.

6

MASAKU

A DREAM COME TRUE

For years I had struggled under some less-than-ideal circumstances in life and education. What I needed most was basic education in math, reading, and the sciences. Where could I get the start I so desperately needed? Over the months and years, the Meads had faced many challenges with my care, but God always came on the scene and made what was needed happen. He did that especially where it concerned my education.

The Meads' economic status was much lower than it was when Dr. Tim was in private practice in America, so they couldn't consider a private school for me. But then they learned from a staff member at CURE about a school for students with disabilities—Masaku School for the Physically Disabled. This staff member—someone with a disability— had attended the school as a child and now held a respectable position at the hospital. *Perhaps this could be my future as well*, I thought, as I envisioned myself returning to my beloved CURE Hospital to serve others.

It seemed like the right opportunity for me, so Mama Jana made plans to take me there for a visit. Corinne would accompany us.

The day of our visit, I awakened bleary-eyed well before daybreak. All night, I had either dreamed of the day ahead or laid awake staring out the window for signs of first light. As I lay in bed, I plotted the journey we would make through the hills, into the Rift Valley, through Nairobi, and farther away from CURE than I had ever been. With only CURE's grounds and the sounds of children playing in the nearby schoolyard of Kijabe Boys School for reference, I conjured images of the happiest of places.

There would be a sea of students in crisp, blue-and-white uniforms, their faces smiling and their hands raised in class eager to answer questions. Teachers' faces replaced those of nurses as I imagined them enthusiastically educating their pupils. Like there were at CURE, I pictured a team of helpers ready to assist us. What else could *school for the physically disabled* mean but that every need had been anticipated and accommodated?

I also thought of life in the dorm with my classmates. I daydreamed of a band of solid friendships instead of a revolving door of temporary relationships. And instead of a hospital bed, I would have my own quarters, my own things. Mama Jana had been collecting a boxful of supplies for weeks—my very own books, pencils, erasers, shoes, and clothing. I remembered the prophetic words of my village elders. Soon I would be on my way to becoming *akiim*—the doctor.

I couldn't sleep. I was too excited. By 2 a.m. I had showered and dressed, and was awaiting Mama Jana's arrival. Two hours later, she, Corinne, and I loaded into the car. The town of Machakos was 125 kilometers from Kijabe. Our journey would take us four hours across the rough roads of the countryside and through Nairobi's urban traffic jam, with trucks going only five miles an hour.

When we were on the eastern outskirts of Nairobi, the overwhelming smell of diesel fuel made me sick to my stomach. All the while, I sat in the back seat, anxious and impatient.

***

At the school, a watchman opened the compound's tall, blue gate and then sent word of our arrival. The principal met us at the gate and ushered us in. Exiting the car and getting into my wheelchair, I immediately struggled to turn the wheels against the stony earth.

I surveyed the grounds to see no lush, manicured landscaping as there was at CURE. A web of narrow, uneven pathways traversed what had once been a lawn. I watched as children in tattered uniforms pushed classmates propped up in wheelchairs that were too big for them across the grounds. Others in plain clothes dragged themselves on hands and knees through the dust toward dilapidated, tin-roof buildings.

This was the image that would stay with me for the rest of my life. I had lived in a super clean pediatric orthopedic hospital for two years. And I had never before witnessed so many children with disabilities living in such a poor state. It was a pitiable sight. My heart sank. Surely something could be done for disabled people like these. But what could it possibly be?

Concern crept across Mama Jana's and Corinne's faces as we headed toward the boys' housing. Masaku had three dorms—two for boys and one larger building for girls. Each boys' dormitory housed around eighty students. We entered, and immediately the smell of urine assaulted us. Forty bunk beds covered in soiled blankets and packed closely together lined the walls of the dark hall. The bathroom was covered in the grime of human waste. Its toilets and sinks were brown with neglect.

The principal seemed unfazed as he showed us around and introduced us to the dorm mother. This sole woman was in charge of the upkeep of the dorm and the care of its dozens of residents. No wonder this place was not quite up to CURE standards.

I looked up to see tears in Mama Jana's eyes. My heart pounded in fear. We had all been naïve about the realities of a government-run school. The fact was Masaku was the place school districts dumped children with physical and intellectual disabilities when they could not or would not accommodate their needs. Some families paid a fee to enroll their children, but anyone who had a disability was received there regardless of ability to pay. The school was poorly funded, under-resourced, and understaffed.

I had seen a different life at CURE, a different attitude toward people with disabilities. I had nearly forgotten the scourge some societies inflict upon those who are different.

In many ways, this felt like a return to Kakuma. Was I back in that place, "nowhere", with its filth, dust, and stinking latrines? What was I getting myself into? I knew a hospital was no place to live long-term, but was I prepared for an environment such as this? Was this truly a place where I could learn and advance, or would I find myself permanently herded away from society?

"Michael, you don't have to go to school here," Mama Jana told me, ready to walk away. She and Dr. Mead had invested too much in my recovery to leave me in such a place to deteriorate. I had grown accustomed to the luxuries of CURE and the pampering of its staff.

At the same time, though, it had not been so long that I had forgotten what I had lived through in Sudan and at Kakuma. I had survived much worse than this when I was in poorer physical condition than I was now. I thought, too, of so many who remained at the camp, still waiting for medical relief and for an opportunity to go to school. I was learning there is always a struggle to achieve one's dreams. This was mine, and I would make the best of the situation. I would not, could not, miss this opportunity.

"Thank you, Mama Jana, but I can do this." I smiled at her skeptical face.

The principal led us to his office to assess my skills. He knew I had never attended school formally, and he asked a series of simple questions to supposedly determine my academic abilities.

"What is your name?"

"How old are you?"

"What day is it?"

I felt insulted. Did he think I was stupid? I did not want to answer, but Mama Jana gave me a nod of encouragement to cooperate.

The principal determined that I would go into the seventh grade, and that was pretty amazing for someone who had never been to school. It was already September, and the third term of the school year, and students in the eighth grade would be taking exams for the Kenya Certificate of Primary Education in October. I would not have enough time to prepare to join them, thus the assignment into the seventh grade was decided. When I had finished the seventh and eighth grades, I would take the exam, and my score would determine what high school I could attend.

We all agreed that waiting a year ensured my best chance at success. If I did well in seventh grade, I would advance. If not, I would repeat the year to gain more basic academic skills. This seemed a fair plan to me. I was already in my teens, and many of my peers who were a similar age had been delayed in starting school as well. Still, most had more educational foundation than I did. I felt a mixture of intimidation and anticipation as we wrapped up plans for me to enroll and begin my studies.

Mama Jana and I returned to Kijabe to prepare for my departure and for me to say farewell to all who had stepped in as mothers, fathers, and mentors to me over the past two years. On my final night, my CURE family gathered to throw me a party. Then, bearing both hopefulness and trepidation, I was off to begin a new chapter of my life.

***

The Meads arranged for someone to give the bathrooms of every dorm at Masaku a thorough cleaning, and they left a supply of disinfectant. When the teachers saw the results, they begged to have their bathrooms cleaned as well.

Before Mama Jana left, we stripped my bed and put on a set of clean linens. Then when it was time to say goodbye, we both broke down and cried. She cried in fear for my safety and health. I cried because, once again, I was facing loss. Every step toward progress had meant a painful letting go of those dear to me—my mother and siblings, my father and Abraham, and now my CURE family and the Meads.

I was weary—so weary—of loss.

Now I would be forced to quickly learn how to live independently as a young man with a disability. There would be no nurses keeping me company at night, no Francesca and Earnest to encourage me in the Lord, no doctors close by if my health deteriorated. But I had made it through war, life-threatening disease, and life in a refugee camp. I would make it through this place too. I would press ahead toward a goal that once seemed impossible.

Rolling into the dining hall that evening, I saw a series of crude murals on the wall. Painted in both Swahili and

English was the phrase *Ulemavu sio Ukosefu*—"Disability is not Inability." On the opposing wall I read in English, "My disability has opened my eyes to my true abilities." I did not understand these sayings at first. I was still learning to read and write in Swahili, and my English skills were just emerging. But in time I would come to grasp their meanings. They seemed out of place and in contradiction to all that I saw around me. But daily, these words would stand as a counter message to the reality of harsh life at the school.

My first night at Masaku, I tossed and turned in the heat of eighty bodies crammed into one room. Those of us who used wheelchairs slept in the lower beds, while those with more mobility climbed with effort to the top bunks. As I lay awake in misery, I kept rehearsing in my mind the words from the book of Job that Earnest had shared with me from a Swahili Bible: *Lakini mimi najua ya kuwa Mkombozii wangu yu hai*—"I know that my redeemer lives" (Job 19:25). I may have felt alone in that room of strangers, but this was not a God-forsaken place. The Lord would be with me here as he had been with me all these years.

In the morning, our dorm mother awakened us at 4:30 a.m. to take a cold shower and get ready for the day. She could assist only the most challenged among us, and I watched as my dorm mates jumped in to help those who needed assistance with bathing, toileting, dressing, and making their beds. Soon someone was by my side to help me.

When we were done, we quickly made our way outside the building and into the sunshine to warm up and head toward the cafeteria. Meals were the same every day: a bowl of plain porridge in the morning, and bland rice and beans for lunch and supper. I struggled to eat the food at first, but hunger soon brought me to my senses. In time, I learned to give thanks for those meals. I had not forgotten the cramping pain of starvation. Here was food before me, and it was God's provision.

Masaku may have felt like a return to Kakuma, but I would not be stagnant here as I had been there. Instead, this would be a place of personal growth, not only academically but in my maturity and my identity as a young man with a disability. The school also held daily prayer times and worship assemblies, which would aid in my spiritual growth.

As I settled in at Masaku, I began to notice aspects of community life that reminded me of Dinka culture. My fellow students with disabilities and I had few resources and supports, but we survived through a system of teamwork, and no one was left behind to fend for themselves. The boy who needed help with walking leaned against the wheelchair of a friend, and the wheelchair-user found in that companion an assistant to push him across the campus. If one needed help to go to the bathroom, another would take him. If one could not feed himself, another would lift the spoon to his mouth. We were responsible for washing our own clothes, and as I washed mine, another would gladly hang the garment on the line to dry.

My new friends had learned that we would not survive without cooperation, so we moved together as a group. At the refugee camp, and even within my village, I had been isolated in my disability. But here we learned solidarity.

In my year and a half at Masaku, our tightly knit community lost three classmates. Inadequate nutrition and lack of medical attention meant a poor outcome for the weakest and most vulnerable among us. Together, we grieved as a family and comforted one another.

At Masaku, then, I learned important lessons about community and fellowship that would serve me well as a young adult. Even now, surrounded by others with disabilities, I felt my limitations in the chair. Yet I wanted to be as independent as I could. The irony was in how the inaccessibility of the space itself worked against us all. I thought often of the responsibilities that would have been on my shoulders had I been back in my village and not become ill. My life had slowed down immensely from its original trajectory. At Masaku, I wrestled with my discontent and tried to make peace with my new life and identity.

Soon after arriving at Masaku, I developed a friendship with a young man named Dennis. I first noticed him when I arrived at the dorm and learned he did not have a uniform. Mama Jana had packed three for me. In Luke 3:11, I had read that John told a crowd, "If you have two coats . . . give one to the poor. If you have extra food, give it away to those who are hungry" (TLB). I remembered the verse and was prompted to share one of my uniforms with Dennis. This small act won me a faithful friend.

Dennis barely had any physical challenges, and was strong cognitively. But a limp and weakness in one arm had been sufficient for him to be sent away from the regular school system to Masaku. In Africa, even a little disability greatly affects how people are viewed by others and what is assumed about their future.

Like me, Dennis was not from among the Kamba people who inhabited Machakos and the surrounding region. If the other children were speaking their mother tongue, Kikamba, both he and I would be left out of the conversation. So together we forged a friendship communicating in Swahili. Dennis was also my partner in mobility. During the week, he would meet me at the end of class to push my chair across the rocky schoolyard. On wash day, he would be right by my side to assist me. Dennis had found his purpose at Masaku—that of a helper.

Arriving at Masaku toward the end of the school year, I was highly motivated to learn, but I had only the most basic of academic skills. I could not yet write well, and I was not proficient in either English or Swahili. But I found my teachers, though overwhelmed and overworked, to be kind and dedicated to their students, making the best of the few resources available to them. Classes crept ahead at a slow pace as staff worked to help the most academically challenged among us keep pace.

Here again, I needed to rely on my own determination to learn and on the help of my classmates to succeed.

Studying hard helped distract my mind from hunger pangs and the poor circumstances around me.

I excelled in math. The Dinkas knew math! We counted our cows: how many we had amassed, how many were needed for a bride price, how many had gone missing. If a man had three daughters getting married, and each groom gave him two hundred cows, he knew well how his herd would increase.

Earnest and Francesca had prepared me for religion class, and I did fairly well in history class. But I barely passed the other subjects, and was at the bottom of my seventh-grade class. I had scored just well enough to advance to eighth grade, and was disappointed in myself.

I was also frustrated with my progress in Swahili. At best, I could speak only a broken language. At the hospital, I had never heard or seen many of the words I now encountered. But though I was doing poorly in her class, my Swahili teacher saw my potential and became my best encourager. "I think you are going to make it, Michael," she would say. And I would work hard to prove her right.

Titus was the smartest boy in our class, finishing first in seventh grade. He had cerebral palsy, and that limited movement on one side of his body. It also affected his speech. Cognitively, however, he was clearly advanced. He was another student who, because of a mild physical disability, had been denied the opportunity to study in the regular school system with its better resources.

Titus's disability had cost him more than a better education. As a young child, his father, ashamed of his son's differences and believing him to be cursed, had abandoned the family. Someone in the community took Titus from his overwhelmed mother and brought him to Masaku. This school and its community of students was the only home and family he knew. Here he had found acceptance and confidence. Here he had learned to excel. His teachers took note of his advanced abilities . . . and so did I.

I was happy to find that he wanted to be friends and to help the new boy—me—to acclimate. But he was also sizing me up. Was I competition? Yes, that was certainly my intention. He asked me about my school history and laughed to learn this was my first experience. "If you study hard, you will do OK," he offered condescendingly. He was not concerned, but he had miscalculated.

Titus became my challenge. He had been top boy since first grade, and I intended to topple him from glory. Our teachers picked up on our friendly rivalry and encouraged it. We pushed each other. I studied hard even on my breaks from school. By the end of the first term of eighth grade, I had achieved second place among my peers. By the second trimester, I was in first place.

In eighth grade, I revived my role as ambassador, sharing the message of hope with my fellow students. As one of the older students, I became a role model for studying hard, making the best of the situation, and keeping a positive outlook. I became head boy, keeping an eye on the younger students, shifting my concern from my own needs to those now under my care. I wanted to be a good servant leader.

7

HOME TO MY CURE FAMILY

My first extended break from school came in December of 2007, and I counted the days until I could escape the grounds of Masaku and retreat to Kijabe. However, that first Christmas when I went home to CURE Hospital, the Meads were not there. They had traveled to the United States to be with their family.

Instead of finding Kenya a peaceful reprieve, it was reeling amid a contentious election. Opposing candidates had both declared themselves victor, and neither was willing to concede. This led to weeks of civil unrest and tribal hostility. Angry protestors took to the streets of Nairobi and other major cities with machetes and torches, burning the communities of rival tribes. Hundreds were killed, and hundreds of thousands were displaced. From the safety of the heights of Kijabe, I could see a hillside filled with the tents of those who had fled for refuge from the violence. I wrestled with painful flashbacks to my life in Sudan. War, it seemed, had found me again.

Though anxious and preoccupied by national events, and despite the Meads not being there, it was good to be back with my CURE family for a few weeks. Once I had longed to escape the confines of this hospital. Now I was thankful to be safe within its walls again, to eat wholesome meals, regain some weight, and enjoy a bit of spoiling from my friends.

In January, Kenya settled its political dispute and formed a coalition government. Conflict across the country subsided. I returned to Masaku to complete my final year of study, determined to do well in the national exams.

***

When the April break came, I got my first real opportunity to learn about my newly adopted Mead family. In the hospital, my interaction with the Meads had been limited. I would see Dr. Mead mainly as he made his daily rounds. He was *Daktari* to me, and our relationship was as doctor and patient. Jana was Mama Jana, but "mama" is a term of respect for mature women in my culture. I knew her as the kind woman who visited me at my bedside and in the playroom to help me learn to read and to encourage me in Christ.

So when God touched their hearts to assume care for me, it was a complete surprise. Up until that time, this had not been the nature of our relationship.

The Meads came to visit me at Masaku on parents' weekends. They took me out for *chipatis*—a thin, flat bread—and sent me back to campus with a box of them for my dorm mates. They were generous people, thinking not only of me but of the other children in need at the school. I loved and appreciated them dearly, and they had abundantly displayed their love and commitment to me. But there was still much I did not know about them. I saw myself more as a recipient of their charity than a member of their family.

The Mead home in Kijabe was within walking distance of CURE Hospital, and a small community of missionaries and Kenyan medical staff serving the hospital lived nearby. I had not spent any significant time at the Mead home previously because it had not been accessible by wheelchair. So I had been content to stay at the hospital when not at Masaku, and I did not expect to be welcomed into their household. But I was. Now, at my spring school break, the Meads wanted me *home*.

I arrived to find that in the months I had been at Masaku, they had worked thoughtfully to set up their house to accommodate me. They had installed a ramp at the front door for my wheelchair. Inside, furniture had been rearranged to clear paths for me to pass from one room to the next with ease. Then Mama Jana led me to the bedroom she had prepared for me, thinking through every need for my comfort, making the space mine. But that's not all. The Meads had also made space in their hearts and private lives for me.

It took time for me to truly understand this. I had not been *home* for years. I had dreamed of returning to my village, of seeing Mama's and Baba's faces again, and of sitting together with my siblings outside our hut. That had been my heart's longing. But I could not go back to that life. Instead, the Lord had provided this new home and a second family. I was being welcomed as a son. There was rest here! There was love!

It was just *Daktari*, Mama Jana, and me at home for much of that first break. Their three adult children were living in the United States, and their teenage daughter attended a local high school during the day. We spent our three weeks together learning about one another and sharing about our lives. I learned what drove the couple's lives of service.

Mama Jana was the anchor of the family. While Dr. Mead worked as a surgeon at CURE Hospital, she was busy managing the household and serving the Lord in her own missionary ventures. At the hospital, she had taken on the ministry of prayer for both the staff and patients. Down the hill in the valley, she had started a feeding program that provided meals to preschoolers. She had partnered with a local Maasai activist to raise support for a home and school for girls rescued from early marriage and female genital mutilation. Together, they also assisted widows in starting small enterprises making uniforms and washable sanitary products. And she taught a team of Indian ladies to quilt, using it as an opportunity to share Christ.

Mama Jana connected many people to ministries in the United States, and she helped raise awareness and funds to support and grow indigenous organizations. She even helped my uncle Abraham realize his dream of studying nursing in Uganda so he could then return to South Sudan to help people there. I came to see her as a sort of a saint—a superwoman. I marveled at all she was able to do. But she was always quick to give credit to the Lord. She worked for his glory and in his strength. God would show her a need and move her heart to act in love.

I was swept up in Mama Jana's love. She told me she and Dr. Mead had observed how I faced setbacks at the hospital, and how in time they had seen me push past my own pain to encourage other patients. I was surprised that they had talked about me at home. Their hearts had been warming toward me for months. Once, Mama Jana had desired to adopt a Kenyan baby, but Dr. Mead was wary of taking on the care of an infant at their stage of life. So the Lord had shown his sense of humor: he gave them a teenager!

During our weeks together, Dr. Mead carved out time in his schedule to spend with me. He took me on trips down into the Rift Valley and to the town of Mai Mahiu near Mount Longonot National Park. There we saw the park's animals, such as zebras, antelope and deer of all kinds, and hippos.

While traveling on these trips, Dr. Mead shared about his life and what had brought him and Mama Jana from the United States to Kenya. Like Mama Jana, he wanted to serve God by serving others. He had been a successful orthopedic surgeon in Michigan when the Lord called him. With little hesitation, he left his practice and a comfortable life behind. Together, he and Mama Jana packed up their kids and moved from an affluent lifestyle to rural inland Kenya. We talked about my surgeries and the miracle of my recovery. He joked that he knew me "inside and out."

I was struck by the way he loved others so deeply. At the hospital he was called *Mzee*, which means "elder"—a father figure. Everyone looked up to him as a role model. Years later, I came to understand the Lord's good plan in placing me in the Mead home. Their gift of love and hospitality extended way beyond my own needs, and their missionary drive planted a seed in my heart to return to serve my people with practical help and gospel hope.

The Mead marriage was my first experience with a Western marital union. Among the Dinka, marriages were arranged, transactional, and utilitarian. They were a way for a man to build wealth. A wife might be one of many wives in a family. Couples shared love and commitment, but war placed intense stress on marriages. Husbands and wives like my parents rarely saw each other as they strove to protect and provide for their families. And while my mother's faith was strong, the cruelties of war had caused my father to struggle to hold on to his.

In the Meads, I saw partners working toward a common mission. Their shared love for God strengthened their love for each other and compelled them to love and serve others.

***

Back at school with the Kenya Certificate of Primary Education examination approaching, I studied hard in the remaining terms. Titus and I continued our friendly rivalry, pushing each other toward the finish line. In November of 2008, I sat the final exams, and the following month I graduated from Masaku School for the Physically Disabled. It had been a hard testing ground for me but also an opportunity. As I struggled, I emerged stronger and more self-confident than ever before.

On graduation day, I found myself deeply torn. For a year and a half, I had longed for vacations when I could escape the school grounds to the good food and comfort of Kijabe. Now I was reluctant to say goodbye. This goodbye was not for a three-week break; it was permanent. I had risen among my peers as a leader. I once pitied the sight of my fellow students, but I had come to embrace my identity as one of them. I saw them as capable, brave, resilient, and loyal. At Masaku, we had seen one another as valuable—even essential to each other. We were bonded as a community. I had made great gains in the classroom, but my peers had taught me just as much. I had struggled to adapt to life in a wheelchair, but I had also learned the beauty of interdependence. We were a family.

I wondered who would lead the younger children once our class graduated. At the final assembly, I thanked my teachers and pledged to return. I felt the weight of my responsibility to this place. My heart was burdened for Masaku and its children. It had all become part of me.

I was also concerned about friends like Titus who were graduating and had no family awaiting their return. What would Titus's future be like? Perhaps he would go on to Joy Town Secondary School—another government-run institution like Masaku but for high school students.

Joy Town was not the best option for me, however. The Meads were determined that I should attend college, so they wanted me to have the most ideal high school education possible. Mama Jana had been making calls, but with little promising results to date. So as I rode for the last time through the blue gate of Masaku, I wondered what my own future held. If I had done well in national exams, this would open many doors for me to gain admission to the best high schools in Kenya. But another factor had to be considered: few schools could accommodate me in my wheelchair.

With Christmas approaching and the Mead children returning to Kenya for the holidays—the adult children flying in from the United States—I turned my attention to getting to know my new extended family.

The Meads had planned to travel to the Kenyan coastal town of Mombasa for a few days of recreation in December. While I was eager to meet their adult children, I was reluctant to be included in vacation plans because I didn't want to be a bother. Why should they spend their vacation taking care of me? But Mama Jana would not hear of my staying in Kijabe. She had been planning this trip for months. And now that I was home from school, they would see about getting me a passport. Without one, I could not fly.

Like many refugees, I had arrived in Kenya with no official documents. At best, my birthdate and age had been approximated. To obtain a passport, I would need a birth certificate. The Meads reached out to Uncle Abraham, still at Kakuma, to ask him to travel to the city of Bor, in South Sudan, for the necessary document. They would fund his travel expenses.

He welcomed the mission. It was late 2008, and there was a period of relative calm in South Sudan. There had been a cease-fire as the people prepared to vote for either an independent South Sudan or to remain united to the Sudan in the north. It was a hopeful season for the Dinka people. The raids had finally ended. Independence, the very thing for which they had suffered, seemed within grasp. This was Abraham's first opportunity to travel home safely to the family.

When Abraham returned with my birth certificate, he also brought back news of my parents and siblings, about whom I had heard nothing in years. They were safe and well. With a reprieve from the conflict, they had been able to establish themselves in one location. Their lives were not perfect, but there was peace. I also learned that my mother was expecting again. I was overjoyed even as my heart yearned to see them all. Abraham had given them a picture of me. They could see that I was healthy, well cared for, and out of danger. They celebrated to hear that I had been attending school and had found a life with the Meads.

With my birth certificate in hand, Mama Jana and I went to the Sudanese Embassy in Nairobi. Immediately, we encountered resistance. The guards would not allow us to even enter the compound without photos. I could see Mama Jana's frustration; it had been a long journey to be immediately turned away. And then when we found the place where photos could be taken, there was no wheelchair accessibility.

Eventually, we removed the wheels from my chair just to enter the building. I felt embarrassed and a burden. I did not want Mama Jana making this fuss on my behalf. But finally, we got the photos and were able to meet with an official at the embassy to get my application processed.

The officials told us it would be another month before my passport would arrive. Waiting a month would ruin the plans for me to go with the Meads to Mombasa. Mama Jana pleaded with the official. She poured out the story of my illness and journey to Kenya, my surgeries, and the miracle of my survival. A half hour later, the official returned with a crisp new passport. Mama Jana broke down and cried. Again, we had seen the Lord's grace.

In Mombasa, I experienced the ocean for the first time. I knew the White Nile, which flows through South Sudan—its name coming from the clay sediment carried in the water. But the sight of the Indian Ocean was overwhelming. Its deep blue spread out as far as the eye could see, with somewhere the intense blue of the sky blending seamlessly with the intense blue of the water. Waves rolled in and crashed on the beach. I'd had no idea the ocean made that kind of sound when it came ashore. It was amazing! It was wonderful. And I could not get enough of the experience. "I have never seen a child smile so much," a woman at the resort remarked.

Those days together with the Meads and their children sealed in my mind the place I had in their family. The children readily welcomed me. The oldest daughter, Becky, had just finished at Trinity College of the University of Toronto. Ben had finished studying to be an engineer at Calvin College in Grand Rapids, Michigan. Aaron was attending college at North Park University in Chicago. The youngest daughter, Abby, was still studying at the Rift Valley Academy in Kenya.

I was not just a recipient of the Meads' charity, as I had feared. I was one included, accommodated, and integrated into their lives. I was family.

8

HILLCREST

ON TO GREATER THINGS

That December, my results for the Kenya Certificate of Primary Education arrived. I had scored well enough to attend my choice of Kenya's college preparatory schools. Even though I had studied hard to prepare, I was surprised by my success.

Mama Jana resumed her search for a secondary school, but not even the American school, Rift Valley Academy in Kijabe, would be able to receive a student in a wheelchair. Then we learned of one more school: Hillcrest Academy, a private British secondary school in Nairobi. They had previously accommodated a student in a wheelchair and were surprisingly eager to receive me.

As we toured the campus with the headmaster, we discussed installing ramps, widening doors, and the various ways spaces could be retrofitted to allow accessibility for a wheelchair-user. In addition, the school would offer me a scholarship reducing tuition fees by half. I was grateful and amazed by their generosity, and yet again I was overwhelmed by God's answer to prayer.

I arrived on campus in early January of 2009, and the experience was very different from when Mama Jana dropped me off at Masaku. There were no tears this time. I was just nervous and excited and determined to do my best. Cars lined the street outside the dorm as diplomats, businessmen, and the elite from across Africa and the world moved their children on to campus. I had lived many lives in my sixteen years, but this place produced culture shock. African, Indian, and European students moved in and out of the buildings greeting each other in English. I had never before encountered such a diversity of people. How could I keep up with such well-educated international students?

Cheerful dorm parents welcomed the Meads and me, and directed us to my private room. Sunlight streamed in through the glass window and lit up the white walls. A clean mattress awaited the new sheets Mama Jana had purchased for me. These had been the quarters I had imagined finding at Masaku but had not. Now they felt almost intimidating. There was a lounge with a T.V., access to a gym and pool, and a private dining hall serving the best foods. And because the dorm had its own laundry facilities, no longer would I wash my clothes by hand and hang them out to dry.

I thought of the great contrast with the life so many of my friends still endured at Masaku. Here students lived and studied in comparative luxury. I felt as though I had moved from zero to ten in a very short period of time.

It was the middle of the school year, and once more I had missed the first semester of classes because Hillcrest followed the British term times, this time beginning in grade ten. I was also behind my peers because I had again skipped several grades and so had missed essential preparatory work. In the first weeks, I discovered how much I did *not* know. Another challenge was that everyone spoke English here. I had learned *some* English at CURE and had practiced with the Meads, but at Masaku I had spoken Swahili exclusively. Here, few people spoke Swahili even recreationally. I would have to learn English and learn it quickly.

I would also have to figure out how to navigate the campus and its buildings. Unlike Masaku, where I was in one classroom for the entire day, at Hillcrest I would move from class to class. I had doors to open, hills to get up and down, and ramps to maneuver in my chair, all while learning my way around.

My first class, English, was taught by an instructor with a British accent so thick that I missed two thirds of what she said. In my IT class, our instructor said, "Log in to your computers." I watched as my peers confidently typed away. Log in? How? I had never typed or used a computer before. I returned to my dorm room exhausted yet excited. Everyone seemed so far ahead of me with the most basic of skills. I doubted my ability to catch up, yet I wanted this so badly. It would be a challenge, and I welcomed it!

At Masaku, I had been able to shine in my academic abilities and leadership skills, and there was nothing out of place about my wheelchair. No one prejudged me because of it. It created no barriers to building relationships. But here the chair made me glaringly obvious to some and invisible to others. My disability was the first thing anyone noticed about me. I was self-conscious.

I was also pretty sure I was among the poorest students in the school. As well, my peers knew the world. They were up to date on global events, and had their own opinions and experiences for which I had no reference. I felt embarrassed by my naiveté. My life had been lived in the bush, in a refugee camp, on a hospital bed, and in the confines of a dilapidated school.

"What does your father do?" they would ask. "Was he a doctor? Or perhaps he was in the government or a diplomat?" How could I answer? How could I tell them he was a poor farmer? How could I say he was a *beny* fighting for the freedom of his home country? I couldn't even be sure Baba was still alive. They were shocked to learn that I had attended school for only a year and a half. But at that time, I was too young to grasp the weight of my personal history and testimony. I did not want my background to be a hindrance. I just wanted to fit in.

I applied myself to my work, but it took me five times as long to grasp material others understood at once. I fought for every passing grade, and I needed my classmates' help if I were to survive the semester. Wherever a group of the smartest among my peers gathered, I would wheel up to join the conversation. *Walk with the wise and become wise*, I thought. At first, they ignored me with my broken English, but I strove to be as friendly as I could. I needed to listen in and pick up what I could to help me catch up. As I grasped math, I would contribute my own wisdom to the discussions. In time, some students began to include me.

My teachers were supportive, recognizing the effort I was making. The Meads purchased a computer for me, and I practiced on it daily, first typing out my name as fast as I could. At the end of my first semester, I barely passed to advance, but I had done well in math, and I enjoyed learning IT. I had done enough to continue with biology, but I had to drop physics. I was disappointed by my grade.

The Meads were very understanding. In the same way they always had, they helped me keep perspective and see things positively. Increasingly, Dr. Mead took on the role of a father. He listened to me and asked questions that helped me think through my concerns. He guided my development.

I kept my head down and focused on my schoolwork at Hillcrest. I knew how much the Meads were investing in my education. I knew, too, what grace it had been to be accepted and given the opportunity to study there. For many, the work came easy; they barely had to study. Others who had never known lack took their education lightly and dabbled in as much mischief as they could. But I knew I could entertain neither attitude. I had to avoid trouble. There would be no second chances for me.

In time, I developed a close circle of friends. Azzam was brilliant at math and IT, and was always willing to help me understand hard concepts. Basit, James, Adebo, and I took the same classes in grade eleven. We studied together and pushed one another to stay focused on our work.

Adebo and I could not have come from more different backgrounds. He was the well-educated son of a Nigerian diplomat who worked for the UN in Nairobi. In time, I learned why he found it easy to accept and befriend me. His mother had developed a leg-length discrepancy following a childhood bout of polio, but her deformity had not limited her. She had gone on to attend college, have a family, and pursue a diplomatic career. She had taught her son to assume the value and potential of all people.

Another close friendship I formed was with Gideon, who was a year ahead of me. I had not noticed his disability at first. When he wore a sweater, few could recognize the weakness in one of his arms. But eventually I could. He reminded me of Dennis, my friend and helper at Masaku. Gideon became like a big brother to me. We lived together in the dorm, and like Dennis, he wanted to help me in any way I needed. He introduced me to watching soccer on television, and we bonded over the sport. But there was more to our bond. It is often true that a person with a disability more readily sees and affirms the humanity in others.

Through my friendships with Adebo and Gideon, I was able to gain access to and acceptance from several able-bodied peers. But one event seemed to fling open the doors at Hillcrest for me. At the end of class each day, I exited the educational building and let my wheelchair roll freely down the sloping pavement toward the bank of lockers. One day, Rahul, a boy from my class, joked that he wanted to race me down the hill. Those around quickly joined in challenging us to do it, and we agreed to meet at the next break.

I arrived to find a large group gathered to watch. Someone called, "Ready! Set! Go!" and we were off. I gave the push rims a hard shove, propelling the chair forward, gaining momentum down the hill. I had not considered how I would break my descent at the end of the race, so I found myself careening toward the lockers. My head slammed into the metal as the gathered group cheered. I won the race, but I looked up to see the displeased face of one of my teachers.

I wasn't going to let anything dampen my victory, though—not even a disgruntled teacher. I had impressed my peers. No longer would they see me as fragile and incapable. I had earned their respect. From that day on, I would be *Michael* to them, no longer simply "the boy in the chair."

***

While I was gaining friendships, I could find little fellowship in one area. Hillcrest was a secular school. Gone were the daily prayers and worship assemblies I cherished at Masaku. Those times of spiritual focus had kept us all looking to God. Here at Hillcrest, a wide diversity of religions was represented, and no effort was made by the school to promote any of them. Worship was a private matter rarely spoken of among my peers. Nor could I leave campus to connect with local churches, and there were no spiritual mentors for me among my teachers.

I was timid to share about my faith. Who would listen to me as an authority on God? After all, I was among the least educated of my peers. I would also have to rely on personal study and having a consistent devotional time to sustain me. But I struggled to remain focused on the pursuit of a deeper relationship with God.

One Sunday, I watched as cars pulled up to campus and a group of Westerners emerged. It took me a while to learn about it, but a small Vineyard church met each week right on campus in the school's assembly hall. The Lord had provided! The next Sunday, I wheeled myself over to join them. It was a different environment from the traditional Kenyan services I had attended before. Their music was a new sound to me, and the preaching was a different style. I embraced it all, and they welcomed me. This little congregation of believers helped me sustain my faith during my years at Hillcrest.

At the end of eleventh grade, I sat the O-Level exams. I was nervous. Had I passed *any* subject? There had been so many courses, so much information to process and regurgitate. Had I done enough? I needed to pass 70 percent of my classes to advance to A-Level study and have a chance at a good college. English language and the sciences remained a struggle for me. Even in IT, which I loved, I had fought for every good grade.

I took the tests just before the school year ended, then returned to the Mead home for summer vacation. Mama Jana, always the one to be thinking ahead and planning, was eager to purchase my uniforms for the next term. But I wanted her to wait because I did not share her confidence. Our exams had been sent to the UK for grading, and it would be weeks before we would know my results.

I was a nervous wreck driving back to Hillcrest to get my results. I was afraid of failure and of disappointing the Meads. Repeating a class would be an embarrassment, and it would mean the loss of the community of my classmates. I rolled nervously into the secretary's office, and she handed me an envelope. Afraid to look, I gave it to Mama Jana.

I watched her face as she opened the envelope and began to read. Then she smiled. "You did great, Michael." She handed me the letter. I had achieved surprisingly high marks and passed all my subjects. "Let's go get my uniforms!" I said.

But first we would go to America to check out colleges.

9

A VISIT TO AMERICA

My time at Hillcrest Academy was coming to an end, and it was time to think seriously about where I would go to college. Should I apply to schools in Kenya? Should I think about college in America? America would be great, but it seemed so far away and so big. Where should I start?

I increasingly thought about my newly formed homeland of South Sudan and my potential role there. My thoughts shifted to studies beyond Hillcrest and to a future career in the public sector. Education was the key to life in unlocking such opportunities.

The Meads were determined that I should attend a U.S. university, as their biological children had done. So it was best, they thought, that I travel to America that summer to familiarize myself and lessen the culture shock that would certainly occur the next year. They would take me to their home state of Michigan, and from there we would tour several colleges. And so I went to America with them and began looking at colleges.

The flights to the United States were long . . . and seemed unending. But I was highly anticipating all that lay ahead of me. On the second flight from Europe to the States, the day seemed to be perpetual as we flew with the sun. When we arrived in Chicago, friends of the Meads greeted us and loaded us into their vehicle for another long trip to Muskegon, Michigan. It was summer, and I was surprised to find it was still daylight as we drove away from O'Hare airport at 8 p.m. This was so different from what I was used to in Kenya. At the equator, daylight and darkness are almost the same length all year long.

I was amazed by all I was seeing: the roads paved so smoothly, the highways so wide, massive trucks speeding past us. We stopped at a drive-through, fast-food restaurant. "What do you want, Michael?" I was asked. There were so many choices. A voice appeared asking for our order, and then our meal was waiting for us minutes later at another window. I was amazed by the technology.

We arrived at the Mead home along Lake Michigan. I couldn't stay there, though, because the house was inaccessible for my chair, so the Meads had arranged for me to stay at their friends' more accessible house. Settled in and exhausted, I slept well.

The following morning after breakfast, my hosts encouraged me to explore the community. I wheeled myself down their driveway and out to the sidewalk at the end of their yard. I loved the feeling of the crisp early summer air against my face. My chair moved unencumbered along the paved path of the quiet neighborhood, and curb ramps eased my transition to the roadway. At the end of the avenue was a school closed for summer break. I spotted a running track and made my way to it for a spin.

This was freedom. In the days ahead, I was amazed by the forethought given to making spaces accessible for wheelchair-users. Ramps to enter buildings were everywhere. Doors opened automatically or at the touch of a button. The doorways were wide enough to enter with ease, and in the public bathrooms the sinks were low enough to reach. There were fewer stairs here too. And there were elevators. Beyond educational opportunities, I could imagine a life of independence in America.

***

Our college tour began at three Michigan schools: the University of Michigan in Ann Arbor; Michigan State University in Lansing; and a small, private Christian school, Calvin College, in Grand Rapids, Michigan (later called Calvin University). While Calvin was a Christian school and near the Mead home, Dr. Mead and Jana counseled me to think about the winters, especially in Western Michigan with its deep, lake-effect snowfalls. As I looked at photos of snow and snow and more snow, I began to wonder if I, having been raised in a country just eight degrees north of the equator, could survive a winter anywhere in Michigan—especially in a wheelchair.

The two state universities, which were huge, were in the same snowbelt as Calvin College. I hadn't forgotten those pictures of a Midwestern winter, and it would probably be even more difficult to navigate the larger campuses. We really did need to explore school options with a different climate.

My hosts' daughter, Alicia, lived a thousand miles away in Baton Rouge, Louisiana, where she lived barely ten minutes from the Louisiana State University campus. She would be coming home to visit her parents soon, and when she arrived, I was eager to ask her questions about LSU and Louisiana. The conditions in Baton Rouge seemed ideal: warm weather most of the year and short, cool winters. And most years, no snow. There would not be time to travel to LSU during this month-long visit to the States, but I had heard enough to put LSU at the top of my list.

Could I get in? There was no way to know except to apply. I would do that as soon as I returned to Hillcrest. Only God could make my acceptance happen. Only he knew my heart's desire. It was all up to God.

***

After the month in America, I returned to Kenya to complete my education at Hillcrest Academy. The Meads had accepted an assignment in the United Arab Emirates, so they were no longer nearby, and I was truly independent for the first time. In the twelfth grade, I would have my choice of fewer subjects in preparation for A-Levels. I chose Math, Economics, and IT. They were among the hardest courses but also my favorite subjects. I wanted to challenge myself. I also set about preparing to sit the U.S. SAT examination—a standardized test used to evaluate all applicants' suitability for college admission. For the first time, I felt as though I was starting on an even plane with my peers. They no longer had any academic advantage over me. I was not behind.

During my time at Hillcrest, I had befriended the only other two Sudanese students enrolled. The brothers were younger underclassmen, and they looked up to me as a big brother. I was eager to meet their father. Mr. Abel Moses Majok had led as a general in the Sudanese People's Liberation Army. Now he served as a diplomat representing the Southern people's cause for independence. It had been rare for me to meet someone who understood and witnessed the struggle I had lived through. We did not share a common dialect, but we were fellow Dinka. I was grateful for news from my homeland.

Ambassador Majok shared with me his high hopes for a peaceful and prosperous South Sudan, and he told me of ongoing negotiations toward achieving independence. He was confident the South would prevail. When it did, South Sudan would need educated men and women to invest their time and skills in its development. The Southern region had always been without basic infrastructure common in the developed world.

I began to consider how my future studies might be beneficial in supporting my people and our country. My economics teacher echoed these thoughts. Did the Lord have a plan to use not only my disability but also my education? Understanding that this God-given opportunity was not just for me and my interests gave new weight to my studies. I was now determined to become an economist.

In the first semester of my twelfth-grade year, Sudan prepared to offer its Southern peoples a referendum. They would be given a choice either to remain united with the North, or to be separate and create an independent South Sudan. There would be a polling station in Nairobi for Sudanese living in Kenya. As I would be eighteen years old by the January vote, Ambassador Majok encouraged me to register to vote.

That January, on my way back to campus after Christmas break, the driver stopped at the station so I could join fellow expatriates in exercising my right to vote. We were all excited! Nervous! We were making history this day. The ballot was a simple form, the choice indicated by either an image of hands clasped in unity or a raised hand signaling separation. After my vote, I dipped my finger in the electoral ink with pride. I never wanted that ink to fade. The vote was tallied, and the people's will was made known. The South had overwhelmingly voted to separate and form its own, independent state.

That July of 2011, the Republic of South Sudan was born, and excitement spread across Africa. Its longest civil war had ended. I longed to be reunited with my family to share this celebration, but on my own at Hillcrest, I had no way of making contact with them. I could only imagine what this victory meant to the Dinka. The toll of the war had been great. So many lives had been lost, so many people displaced, so much of our way of life devastated. But now we had a chance for restoration and peace.

***

In February of my final year at Hillcrest, my classmates and I began to receive letters of acceptance from colleges. When the email arrived from LSU, I was nervous to open it. This was the answer that mattered most to me. I had been determined to choose LSU, but had they chosen me?

"Congratulations!" the letter read. "You have been accepted to Louisiana State University!" I swelled with relief and gratitude. The Lord had opened yet another door for me. Oh, if only I could share this moment with my parents. My acceptance was a pride to be shared by my whole village. I would be the first among them to attend university.

Just a few years earlier, I had not been so sure I would be counted among my graduating class. But now my classmates and I all shared our news of acceptances and plans to continue our studies. Many of them would be attending British schools and continuing their friendships in the UK. I was one of a few who would attend a U.S. school. There had been a running debate as to which system was better. LSU may not have carried the prestige of my peers' choices, but I knew it was the place the Lord had arranged for me. I had also tasted freedom in the United States, and I longed to begin life there.

The weeks flew by as my peers and I, with graduation and college careers in sight, buckled down to study hard for our upcoming final exams. Hillcrest had been a nurturing and refining experience for me. My body had become strong and healthy there. I had been able to recover from years of malnutrition. I had gained new confidence and self-esteem. I had been exposed to a host of new ideas and a broader perspective of the world. I had gained a sense of order and discipline, and I had learned the value of challenging myself intellectually. At this academy, I had been taught to dream. I had entered shy, weak, and unsure of myself. Now I would leave this gate ready to take on the world.

I, too, had made my small mark on this campus. For most of my teachers, this had been their first experience accommodating a student with disabilities. They told me I had opened their eyes and changed their mindset about what is possible. As I prepared to graduate, the school was making progress toward becoming more fully accessible. They were ready to fully embrace new students with needs similar to mine. The time I spent at the school had not been only for my benefit.

The Meads flew from the United Arab Emirates to Kenya for my graduation. The night before the final ceremony, I gathered with my peers for an awards banquet. The guys were dressed up in suits and ties, and the girls wore gowns. We looked like men and women. As we entered, parents, teachers, and faculty applauded. My peers strolled in, and I rolled in, with a jovial and celebratory mood, giddy with excitement and relief. But for me, this moment carried a gravity that others could not fully understand. Had it not been just yesterday that I was a pitiful refugee unable to read or write English? Was it not a short time ago that I was lying paralyzed, unable to get around? Was I that young child staring out from that dark tent at an uncertain future, hoping for an education?

"Thank you, Jesus," I whispered.

I received awards for several subjects that night, including most improved in math and outstanding mentor to younger students. Wheeling up to the stage, I saw my American parents in the audience. They were beaming with pride. The Meads were a huge part of this story the Lord had been writing.

"What problems in the world are you called to solve?" our headmaster challenged us to consider. What indeed did God want me to do? Where would I go? Hillcrest created dreamers. What was the biggest dream I could dream?

10

A CITIZEN OF SOUTH SUDAN

Before I left Africa, I wanted to obtain my South Sudan passport and establish my citizenship in that country. I asked Mr. Majok, who had recently been appointed Deputy Ambassador to Norway, for his help. "Leave it to me, Michael. I will arrange it all."

To my surprise, he also offered to cover the expense. Then he shared my story with officials at the Ministry of Foreign Affairs in South Sudan, and they agreed to assist me. I flew to Juba, the new capital of a new nation: South Sudan. Even though I had been born in South Sudan, I had never been to the capital of Juba. I was excited to be going there.

And so that spring break, right before A-Level exams and without even informing the Meads, I flew *home*. On the short flight from Nairobi to Juba, I thought of my flight on the ground with Baba some seven years earlier, when we had evacuated my sickly frame from a war-torn land to Kenya. I had been in horrific pain, and filled with anxiety and uncertainty about what lay ahead. I was so young and naïve about the world outside my village. On *that* day I could never have imagined *this* day. This flight retraced that first journey across the Upper Rift Valley. Eventually, we flew over Kakuma Refugee Camp, my home for two years, and then we approached South Sudan. I looked through the window and saw a green wilderness. I could not see any roads or homes until we approached Juba. "How many of my people are still alive?" I wondered. The war had taken the lives of two million people and four million more had been displaced. The entire population South Sudan was estimated to be between eight and fifteen million people.

The plane was filled with businesspeople. No doubt, they were heading to Africa's newest country to invest. I could hardly wait to see this free and prosperous South Sudan with my own eyes. But mixed with that joyful anticipation was a measure of fear. I had never known life without fear in Sudan. Except for my trek to Kenya, I had never explored the country outside of rural Bor. When I was a child, the city of Juba had been controlled by the ruling North. Now it was in our people's hands as their proud capital. Yet even though the city looked peaceful from above, I knew it was not. The situation remained volatile. I took deep breaths as the plane began its descent toward the airport.

We flew over the White Nile with its long bridge—Bailey Bridge—spanning the river. I could see streets and buildings. The roads were in a deplorable state—a

◀ Michael at CURE Kenya Hospital with Corinne and Nathaniel, 2005.

Michael with Ramathani, 2007.▶

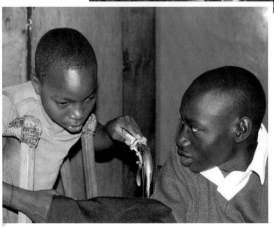

◀ Michael in his school dorm giving his extra sweater to his new friend.

◄ Michael's dorm.

Michael with his classmates and teacher, 2007. ►

◄ Michael's school.

Michael
after being
crowned LSU
Homecoming
King. ▶

◀ Michael with
Rick and Lori
Gerig, Brian
and Mariellen
Boomsma.

Michael with
Joni and Ken
Tada. ▶

◄ Michael with Brian and Mariellen Boomsma.

Michael as a mechanic in Peru. ►

◄ Michael sharing the gospel in Peru.

Michael with Wheels for the World team in Peru, 2017.

◀ First Living
With Hope
team serving
in Kenya,
September 2018.

Chama
crawling
into the
room. ▶

Dr Mead, Dr Theuri and two anesthesiologists, Philis and John.

Masaku students with the team.

◄ Michael meeting
Mama after
14 years, 2018.

Michael sharing at Masaku.

Wheelchair distribution.

Michael with siblings (Martha, John, Elizabeth and Sarah).

Michael with the Mead family.

reminder of the civil war which had finally granted my home country independence and made Juba the capital, but left much of the infrastructure in disarray. Repairing roads and other infrastructure in South Sudan is complicated by the intense amount of rain that falls during the rainy season. The annual precipitation is nearly 1,000 mm (39 in) of rain, mostly falling between April and October. This made working at road building and repair nearly impossible.

The plane eased onto the runway of Juba International airport and I knew I was finally home. It was exciting to land on my native soil after many years. The ambassador met me and assigned a driver to be my assistant for the week. He would take me from my motel to the embassy to process my paperwork, back and forth as necessary. Again, I was flabbergasted by God's grace. The ambassador's assistant transported me to a small motel near the airport. That night I slept in peace in my homeland for the first time ever. The following morning, he drove me to the passport office. From the car window, I felt the familiar hot air of the dry season. The air was full of dust. Along the way, construction workers were taking advantage of the dry season and toiled at new buildings and paved roads. Juba seemed tiny in comparison to Nairobi.

Where will this city be in five years? I wondered. Perhaps it would rival Kenya's best cities and become a hub in eastern Africa. There was the promise of a new and better Juba and South Sudan. However, along the roads, I saw naked boys begging and poor families breaking rocks for gravel with a hammer. Poverty was still evident in this new capital. Juba had attracted poor people from all over the country who were looking for a better life. For many years, fighting and farming had been our people's only occupations. Now the fighting had stopped and the farms had been left in ruins. There was little left for them to pursue in their villages.

At the passport office, South Sudan's new flag flew proudly. Stripes of black and red told of the painful history of our people who had shed their blood to obtain her independence. A green stripe spoke of her natural wealth and resources upon which she would build a hopeful future. White lines signaled the light of peace and goodwill that had come after a very dark season. A blue triangle represented the Nile River, and in its center, a yellow star shone for hope and determination.

Inside the passport office, many people waited to obtain passports and national ID cards. It was good to sit among my countrymen again and to converse in Dinka, however, I struggled to get the words out in my mother tongue. It had been years since I'd spoken the Dinka language, and to hear it pass my lips again left me emotional.

Juba was not wheelchair accessible, so for my week in the city, I was largely confined to the motel. As I sat there all alone, I thought constantly about Mama, Baba, and my siblings. Even though I was so close, I had no way to get to them or even get word to them that I was in the country. I did not know how they fared. Hopefully, tribal conflict had ceased and there was peace back in Bor. No more war and starvation. Perhaps Baba could at last rest. I imagined them all happy, telling stories again around the fire. But I had no way to know for sure.

On my fifth day in Juba, I traveled back to the passport office to collect my crisp, new passport. I sat staring at its pages. I was filled with a newfound national pride. I was Dinka, but I was now also South Sudanese. No longer was I a displaced person, a refugee, or the boy from nowhere. Now I was a citizen of South Sudan.

11

LIFE AT LSU

After graduation from Hillcrest Academy, it was time to move on to the next stage of my life. So many things had happened to me in the last few years. I had started out in Sudan, before it was South Sudan. Then I had moved to Kakuma Refugee Camp for two years. After my time at CURE Hospital in Kijabe, I went to school at Masaku and Hillcrest. Everywhere I went, I met many wonderful people. Now it was time to leave those places and people behind, and to move on to a new life in the United States.

For every step of progress in my life, I had experienced a measure of personal loss. I had said goodbye to my family and villagers in search of a cure in Kenya, I had parted ways with my father at CURE Hospital, and I had left the comfort of my CURE family to attend Masaku. Leaving Masaku, I had lost the security of a community of disabled peers to gain a broader education and perspective on the world at Hillcrest. Now I would leave Africa altogether, and with her, everything that was familiar to me.

I worried that I would lose my very identity in America. But I would come to see that there the Lord had greater plans, greater grace, and a new mission for me. And he himself would be leading me.

In the United States, I would begin to see how the Lord had been working out his plan in my life—how every high and low moment had purpose in shaping me and preparing me to be useful to his kingdom and for his glory. Maria von Trapp, whose story was the inspiration for *The Sound of Music*, once said:

It will be very interesting one day to follow the pattern of our life as it is spread out like a beautiful tapestry. As long as we live here we see only the reverse side of the weaving, and very often the pattern, with its threads running wildly, doesn't seem to make sense. Someday, however, we shall understand. In looking back over the years, we can discover how a red thread goes through the pattern of our life: [it is] the will of God.[1]

I was happy to have finished high school after thinking there was no hope I would even get a small piece of education. But I began to think even more of my successes and my losses as I readied myself to leave for the United States. I thought of South Sudan and my adopted country of Kenya. I wondered if I would ever come back. I wondered if I would ever see my family in South Sudan again. What about the friends I had made at Kakuma

---

1   Maria von Trapp; https://www.azquotes.com/quote/466682.

Refugee Camp in Kenya? And CURE, which had been my home for so many years?

What about Masaku and the deep friendships I had made there? My time at that school had been physically difficult, but I learned there is a harvest in the valley. It was there my faith in the Lord matured.

Hillcrest had its own set of challenges as I schooled with the privileged children of the wealthy. While I had thrived academically at Masaku, I fought for every passing grade at Hillcrest. I struggled, too, to build relationships. I was both glaringly obvious yet painfully invisible. It took time before I found my footing and forged lasting friendships.

These places and people had all impacted my life. Now I must leave them behind. This time I was not going to the United States for a short visit. No, I was moving there and leaving behind everything I knew and loved.

***

After several attempts and many visits to the American embassy, I got my student visa. Then it was time to say goodbye to my continent of Africa. I boarded a one way plane from Kenya to the United States. After the long flight, I then traveled first to Michigan. I needed time to adapt to my new country. Amid all the changes in my life, one sure thing had not changed—the Mead family.

When I first visited the States, I had stayed with friends of the Meads because the Mead home could not accommodate me and my chair. This time I found the Meads had renovated their house—the bathroom was widened, and a ramp went up to the front door. Can you imagine how much money they spent to accommodate me? I felt so loved. The Meads were my family, and I looked forward to coming home from LSU to visit them.

After I'd been in Michigan for a short time, Mama Jana and I boarded a plane headed for Louisiana and my new life.

***

It was August when we arrived in Baton Rouge. Everybody was so friendly and helpful at the airport. But outside, my smile faded away as I immediately realized that, although Kenya could be hot, here in Louisiana it was not only hot but extremely humid. I had never experienced this kind of weather, so I was not used to it. However, Alicia (the daughter of friends of the Meads) was waiting for us, and soon we were in her car. The car's air-conditioning was a welcome relief, just before my clothes got soaking wet from the humidity.

We drove along the Mississippi River. It was a beautiful sight, and I was filled with both anxiety and excitement. Before we arrived at the LSU campus, Alicia showed her hospitality and drove through a local favorite fast-food restaurant, Raising Cane's. Their specialty is chicken fingers, and they were so good I couldn't eat them fast enough.

Soon we were greeted by a huge sign that said: Welcome to Louisiana State University. I whispered to Mama Jana, "After traveling thousands of miles, I am now here. This is something I never thought possible." I couldn't believe it. Again, I was the first person from my village to have the opportunity to attend university. This was more than a dream come true.

I stared out the car window at my new campus—my new home. Located on a plateau of the banks of the Mississippi River, the LSU campus is big and beautiful with oak and magnolia trees everywhere. We arrived at the International Cultural Center, where we were warmly greeted by Maureen Hewitt, the manager of the center. She was like a mother to the international students. She made everyone feel at home. Miss Maureen answered our questions with ease and directed me to my dorm.

When we arrived at the dorm, though, the RAs—the Resident Assistants—student mentors for students living in the dormitories—informed me we were a day early. International students were supposed to arrive a couple of days early, but we were too early, and the dorms were not open for moving in. But I didn't have any other place to stay. I explained my situation, and after a few minutes of consultation, the RAs allowed me to move in and helped me settle into my private dorm room. It wasn't a big job as I had only two suitcases.

Jennie and Arlene, Alicia's friends, had heard I was coming. They had bought bedding, a refrigerator, a microwave, and other things for my room. When they arrived with it all, I was amazed by their kind hospitality. I had everything I needed, and I felt settled.

I was shocked and amazed the next day when other students began to arrive. They had trailers and pickup trucks filled not only with refrigerators, microwaves, and bedding, but with lamps and other stuff as well. I wondered how their dorm rooms could absorb everything they brought.

The next few days were spent in orientation. It was a valuable time because I learned about the campus and met the other students who had traveled thousands of miles to be there. We all had the same goal: to get the education we needed to propel us toward a better future.

With a map in hand, I toured the campus. Tiger Stadium is huge. I couldn't comprehend how many people came there for games. Next to the stadium is the Mike the Tiger Habitat. LSU keeps a live tiger on campus as a mascot. They used to bring him into the stadium on game days, but that is a thing of the past. The Mike the Tiger Habitat is like a park, with lush plantings, a waterfall, a flowing stream that empties into a wading pond, and rocky plateaus. The habitat also has a tower—a campanile.

The campus is big and flat. I thought it would be easy to get around, but I was wrong about that. The roots of those beautiful big trees had pushed up and cracked the sidewalks. The walkways were so uneven that I had to be careful I didn't hit a crack and fall out of my chair or bend the chair beyond use.

Then the big day came for the start of classes. I was excited. I couldn't comprehend what my classes would be like; I just hoped for the best. I was eager to get going, and so were the other students. The hallways were packed with so many students that it was almost impossible to get through them. They were also dressed casually in shorts and T-shirts. At Hillcrest, we dressed up in shirts and ties and coats or sweaters for classes. Casual dress was allowed only one day of the year. So I had on my best shirt, and I felt overdressed.

Not only was LSU big in area but big in the number of students—35,000. I was struck by how huge some of the classes were, with as many as 900 in attendance. The professor would come in, lecture, be recorded for online access, and leave. I wondered, *How can they grade all these students?*

My first day was busy and confusing. I knew which building I needed, but I also had to find the right rooms. I was glad I made it through the day. As if all of this wasn't enough, at the end of the first week, I saw other students checking their smartphones, looking concerned.

"Hey, Michael," one student called. He was still looking at his smartphone. "Do you know a big storm is coming in a couple of days? Hurricane Isaac?"

What? I thought. *What is a hurricane?* We had wind and rain in Africa but not hurricanes. Just what was a hurricane and how bad could it get? And who was Isaac?

Then another student said, "I hope it's not as bad as Katrina."

Isaac? Katrina? Finally, another student explained to me what a hurricane is and how they are named each hurricane season. This one was called Isaac. I did not have a smartphone then, so I had no idea how far away the hurricane was, when it would arrive, and just how dangerous it might be. When I got to my dorm, I looked up hurricanes on the internet. I saw the horrific devastation Hurricane Katrina had caused in this wonderful community. I prayed for safety and asked that the hurricane would not interrupt my new life.

"You better get some food and a flashlight," another student told me. My friend Alicia came and took me to a store where I could gather some food supplies and a flashlight, because it was pretty certain the power would go out. I was so thankful for her help.

Then a strange calm began in the atmosphere. Nothing moved—not a breath of wind. It was the calm before the storm. Soon the wind started, and I could hear it in the roof. It was frightening. Was it going to tear off the roof? But I could do little but pray that the storm would not be too bad. I said to the Lord, *You saved me from so many dangers and brought me here. I trust you will keep me safe. I know you are in control of this storm.*

Hurricane Isaac came ashore with fury. Some electricity went out. Some trees blew down. And there was flooding in some areas. However, it was not as bad as previous storms had been. Classes were canceled for a few days, but soon we were back to a normal life.

Hurricanes, heat, humidity, potentially dangerous sidewalks. This was not what I had expected when I came here to school. I knew I was in the will of God, but I wondered what I had gotten myself into coming to LSU.

***

My English was still not great, but I kept trying to communicate with fellow students. People would start conversations with, "Where are you from?" and I would answer, "Africa." Some would nod and simply say, "Oh." I could always tell which people knew a little about the world and which did not. Africa is a continent—a big continent. Those who knew more about Africa asked, "Oh, what country in Africa?"

In Africa, we often stopped to chat with people, but here we had to stay on a tight schedule. I quickly learned you have to make an appointment to talk with someone.

My classes were going great, but a few things were different. I was accustomed to studying for end-of-term exams. Here at LSU, quizzes and tests ran throughout the term. It took a while for me to understand that all those little quizzes and tests as well as homework contributed a percentage to my final grade.

Some classes were easy, but some were not, and I really had to study hard for them. I had to keep up every day or I would never pass the course.

Another struggle was that some of the buildings were very old and had older elevators that broke down every other day. When that happened, I couldn't get to any of my upstairs classes. It was frustrating, but there was nothing I could do but wait for the elevators to be fixed. And sometimes that took weeks. When I signed up for my next semester's classes, I told the student disability services what had happened with the elevators and the classes. They helped me by moving my classes to suitable buildings. This eased my frustration.

***

In a place like LSU, you can make a lot of friends or you can be lost in the crowd. And to make friends, I had to get out of my comfort zone. America is the land of opportunity, but you have to put yourself out there to take advantage of the available opportunities. I had to do my best to meet people if I was to find my place among the huge crowd of students on campus. Even if I was overlooked by some students as just a guy in a wheelchair, I hoped at least one or two people would know me as Michael.

Matt Redman was one of the first friends I made. I met him my first week of school in our English class. He introduced himself to me, and when I said I came from Africa, he said he was from out of town too . . . from Florida. He said he didn't know a lot of people or have a lot of friends. He invited me to watch an LSU soccer game with him. He also introduced me to his roommates.

Soon my circle of friends began to grow.

***

Then game day came. I had never seen anything like it. People were dressed up in purple and gold—the colors of the LSU Tigers. When I realized I wasn't wearing the team colors, I went back to my dorm and put on my purple shirt. Everyone was dancing, tailgate cooking—

at the back of vehicles, and playing music so loudly you could feel the pulse of the bass. *So this is a college game day!* I thought.

Some of the tailgaters invited me to eat with them. As the sun sank below the bleachers, a sea of football fans who had tickets walked down Victory Hill to the stadium. I didn't go to that first game, but I could hear the loud sound even in my dorm. I wondered what it must feel like to be in the stadium.

The next day everyone was talking about the game. What happened before the game. What happened during the game. What could have happened in the game. And what happened after the game. I felt really left out. So I got serious and decided to learn American football. Matt was a quarterback in high school, and I asked him to teach me some basic rules of the game. He started to explain the positions, the plays, and everything else, but I didn't get it right away. I had thought American football was like rugby, but I was dead wrong.

On the following game day, I decided to go to the game to understand what this hype was all about, and Matt went with me. Once inside the stadium, I was amazed at the number of people in attendance. Crowds at LSU Tiger Stadium average about 102,000 people. You can imagine that the noise was unbelievably loud; my ears were still ringing hours later when I went back to my dorm. When the team came out of the tunnel, the crowd went wild. Fireworks shot up in the air, and smoke from them hung above the stadium. When someone scored a touchdown, people jumped up and down in the stands, some spilling their drinks. The atmosphere was electric.

That night I became an American football fan. And Matt became a true friend and someone who looked after me. Someone who would help me learn about life in America. I no longer felt invisible. Someone was now my friend, and that made all the difference in the world.

***

Everything in Louisiana was different: games, music, food, weather, how people dressed, talked . . . everything. My experience first at Masaku and then at Hillcrest had been hard and a shock to my system. Little did I know those experiences were preparing me for life at LSU.

My first semester was all about getting settled, learning where things were, and figuring out how to get there. I was so uncomfortable with the heat and the size of the campus that for a time I thought about transferring to a school in Michigan. Then, about that time, I joined a campus fellowship, and the students would come to my room for Bible study. Suddenly, LSU began to be doable.

In my second semester I joined a fraternity, Phi Sigma Pi. The fraternity emphasized academics—maintaining at least a 3.0 grade point average—fellowship, and leadership. When I went to the first meeting, I was struck by how friendly and mature everyone was, and I thought I would love to be part of this group. I decided to go to the next meeting, and there I started to get to know some of the members.

Chris Valesquez was the president of Phi Sigma Pi and a nice, humble guy who enjoyed talking to everyone. He was also involved in RUF (Reformed University Fellowship), a Christian organization on campus. When he invited me to a worship night, I went with him out of curiosity, and soon I fell in love with the ministry. RUF became a big part of my faith journey. I regularly attended chapel on campus, and these two places helped build my faith in the secular environment of LSU.

God had provided me a place to belong.

12

THE BURNING BUSH

In the summer of 2013, just after my first year at LSU, I went back to Michigan to spend the break with the Meads. I was thankful to have successfully finished my first year, and it was a relief to spend some time in the cooler air of West Michigan.

The Mead house was situated near Maranatha Bible and Missionary Conference Center, which hosts summer camps. One day not long after I arrived, Mama Jana came into the living room with some interesting information.

"Michael, an event I think you might be interested in is going on over at Maranatha. It's a Joni and Friends Family Retreat for families with children who have disabilities. It's a place where those families can get rest from the constant caregiving. Maybe you should check it out."

I remembered the name Joni. When I was so low at CURE Hospital, Francesca had asked me to come to the playroom to watch a movie. I didn't know English then, so could not understand all of the movie, but I saw a young girl in a hospital who was paralyzed. Then I saw her drawing pictures holding a tool in her mouth.

She also learned to drive a car that had been specially equipped for her. Now, though she was in a wheelchair, she was doing the work of God through her organization, Joni and Friends.

That movie had touched my heart. Way back then I said to God, *If you save my life, I want you to use it like you used Joni's.* So when I heard about the event at Maranatha, I decided to roll across the street and see what was going on at the campground, and if there was a way I could be involved.

"Hello. My name is Michael," I told them when I arrived. "I live right across the street, and I want to know if there is some way I can serve."

A lady who introduced herself as Sandy Hay welcomed me with a warm smile. I learned later that she was the Chicago director for Joni and Friends. Sandy was full of joy, and she loved everyone. She had a passion for the work she was doing.

"I want you to meet someone," Sandy said. She took me to another lady and introduced me. "Mariellen, can you work with Michael at the hospitality desk?"

"Sure," Mariellen answered, and we made our way there together.

People who had questions came to the hospitality desk. Others came to drop off Happy Grams to be sorted and delivered to the campers. Happy Grams are little notes of encouragement people write throughout the week.

I enjoyed working with Mariellen so much. She was kind and sweet and made me feel welcome. She showed me everything on the hospitality desk, and I could tell she was very well organized and a detail-oriented person. She reminded me of Mama Jana. As we started talking, she asked me where I was from, and I told her South Sudan.

"Oh wow!" she said. "My son just ran with the World Vision team, and a young man from South Sudan was on it—he's one of the Lost Boys of Sudan, and a U.S. Olympian. His name is Lopez Lomong."

I was struck by the fact that Mariellen knew about South Sudan, and I felt I could talk with her about my home country. As we spoke, another lady stopped to join our conversation after she heard I was from South Sudan. Her name was Cynthie Haag. Cynthie told me she and her husband went to Sudan in 2005. Her husband, Dr. Jeff, was an ophthalmologist, and they had gone to help people with their vision, volunteering their time. I was moved that she had been in Sudan during the time of war.

These two ladies really showed me their faith in serving the Lord, and I started to open up to them. Mariellen and Cynthie were like family, so I wanted to share my story with them. This was the first time I had talked about my history to anyone since coming to the States.

***

People started coming in with signs and big smiles, and it was time to go back to work as we welcomed families to the camp. Each caregiver held a sign with the name of the family to which they had been assigned. All of these volunteers took care of a child with special needs for the week. There were a lot of hugs and clapping hands as each family arrived. The welcome was incredible, and I was overwhelmed by the love shown to everyone. This was something I had never experienced before.

As I was sorting the Happy Grams the following day, Cynthie asked me if I would like to take a break. "Do you want to ride a horse? Or do the zip line?" she asked.

I was hesitant. "How can I do a zip line?" I had never even thought about doing that. I reasoned, *Being a person with a disability means I just can't do some things, and doing a zip line is one of them.*

"People will be there to help you. You should come," Cynthie said, encouraging me.

I finally said OK.

Soon I was on the go-cart with her, heading up the hill and down the other side to the zip line. I started thinking about what I was doing, and I was nervous. *What have I gotten myself into?*

"Are you ready?" someone asked.

I wasn't sure. "Give me a second." I was trying to buy time, but time was not on my side because I was the next rider. The guys harnessed me up, and soon I was way up in the air. My heart skipped a beat when I looked down. I could hardly see the ground. I mumbled to myself, "Man, I'm scared of heights."

I closed my eyes and took a deep breath. Then they released me, and I flew down the zip line. That day I learned I could do more than sit in a wheelchair. It was *so much fun*, and I didn't die, so I wanted to do it again and again.

I actually felt safe. As a person with disability in Africa I would never have the opportunity to do something like that. After that I was off to ride horseback, go boating, and go tubing as well—where you ride across water on a large inflated tube. These were full and fun days.

***

On Wednesday evening, I rolled down to Lake Michigan to see the sunset. I love sunset time; it is so peaceful. As I sat watching the sinking globe, I saw lots of people at Maranatha playing, smiling, and praising God.

Then suddenly, I heard a voice in my head calling my name. I had never experienced anything like this before—something like Moses had experienced at the burning bush—but I knew it was God's voice. He said, *Look around. What do you see, Michael? This is why I saved your life and brought you this far. These people are created in the image of God, and they are special to me. I want you to observe what is happening here and do this in Africa.*

Right away I wondered how I could ever do that; I could barely take care of myself. So I argued with God. *Lord, I do not see myself as fit for this calling. I'm nobody special. I don't do public speaking, and I haven't got a clue where to start. And besides all this, where would I get the resources? Would people even believe me when I shared my story? Maybe this is not for me.*

After the sun went down, I rode back to the house. Then just before I went to bed, I opened my Bible to the book of Exodus. I knew the story of how God led the people of Israel out of Egypt, but as I read it this time, I had a better understanding. Moses was nobody special when God called him. If God could use an ordinary person like Moses to do extraordinary things, perhaps he could use me too.

I went to bed as God reminded me, *I am God, and with me all things are possible.*

I still didn't really believe I could minister to the disabled, but I told him, *If you want to use me for the good of your kingdom, I will do your will.*

***

Soon the week was over. It had gone by so fast, but my experience at the camp left me with much to think about. I was thankful to have been a part of this special ministry. I went to Sandy Hay on the last day and said, "Thank you and thanks to your team for welcoming me with open arms. This was a life-changing experience for me, and I am thankful to God for letting me be part of the camp."

God had planted a dream in my heart—a dream that would not go away.

13

BACK TO LSU

Soon summer was over and I returned for my second year at LSU feeling renewed by my experience at the Joni and Friends camp. This time I did not live in the dorm but in an apartment on campus. This was more suitable for me because it was quiet, so I could study more effectively, and I could also invite friends to my place on weekends.

I started to experience a deep passion with regard to Africa and the dream God had planted in my heart. I didn't know what to do about it yet, but I decided I would study hard and see what God would do. I also got more involved on campus. I reasoned that if I could do things there to make a difference, maybe one day I could do things other places to make a difference. I wanted to keep God in the center of every decision I made, and it was good to have Christian friends to help me stay solid in my faith.

First Thessalonians 5:16–18 became my theme verses: "Rejoice always, pray continually, give thanks in all circumstances; for this is God's will for you in Christ Jesus" (NIV). I made it a habit to rejoice in everything. I made gratitude to God for my life and opportunities a daily part of my life. And I always tried to smile.

This is how I wanted to live.

***

While at LSU, I realized three things were holding me back out of fear, and it was time for me to come to terms with them. My fear stemmed from first, being a person with a disability, second, being an international student, and third, being a person of color. I felt like a second-class person. I questioned my own value and worth. I felt I didn't deserve opportunities, a happy life, and so on. And for the most part, I felt shunned.

BEING A PERSON WITH DISABILITY

Even though America had made great strides toward putting in place helps for those with disabilities, LSU still had physical barriers to educational services. For example, there was a lack of ramps, elevators didn't always work, and there were heavy doors to open and inaccessible washrooms.

A negative stigma also existed, which was shown through avoidance and/or belittlement. It seemed that many students without disabilities felt superior to those with them. And although some meant well, their pity and overly sympathetic comments and actions could impact the self-view of the person with disability. This put a strain on normal social interactions in and outside the classroom.

BEING AN INTERNATIONAL STUDENT

I sometimes thought, *I am "different." I don't belong here. I am just a guest. I don't have the same rights domestic students do.* Even though my English had improved dramatically during the year and a half that it had been my primary language, I still struggled. And other cultural barriers caused feelings of isolation and loneliness. But I had done my best to adapt to different ways of teaching and learning. I felt I had a responsibility to work hard to overcome these challenges, and I tried my best to blend into this community.

BEING A PERSON OF COLOR

Until the federal courts mandated full integration for LSU in 1964, the school had been segregated. There has been a huge change at the school since then; for example, some of my classes were held in a building named after a civil rights activist. But when I was there, some minority black students were still experiencing racism from the white students. Racist comments made to black students included "Go back to Africa," "Go back to the ghetto," and "Go back to a black school." These comments were hurtful and continued to divide our beautiful campus. Indicative of the problem was a conversation I had with a young white woman. She said, "You are very nice. This is the first time I've ever talked to a black person." That showed me there was much work to be done.

I had previously experienced tribalism, but racism was new to me. With the words of Dr. Martin Luther King

Jr. ringing in my head, I wanted LSU to be a place where students would "not be judged by the color of their skin, but by the content of their character." I decided to be a part of the change.

***

In December of 2013, I heard President Kiir of South Sudan had accused his former deputy, Riek Machar, and ten others of attempting a coup. Fighting broke out and ignited a civil war. Before it was over, an estimated 400,000 people were killed, and more than four million people had been displaced. About 1.8 million of those were internally displaced, and about 2.5 million fled to neighboring countries, especially to Sudan and Uganda.

My heart ached every day as I watched the news, and I saw horrific images on a *60 Minutes* T.V. special on South Sudan. The towns were littered with dead bodies, and the UN had discovered two mass graves. The UN began investigating these incidences as possible crimes against humanity. It was once again a difficult time in South Sudan, and I was deeply distressed for my people. I had many sleepless nights as I thought of my family. I tried to contact them and other relatives for any news, but I could reach no one—although, as you'll see in chapter 19, my family had made it to a refugee camp in South Sudan.

Why did our government commit this horrific genocide? We fought for so many years to have our freedom, but this was what our own government did to our country and to our people. Why? Why? I prayed, *God, please save my family.*

I went back to school in the spring of 2014 with a heavy heart as I still hadn't heard any news about my family. So I kept myself very busy with schoolwork, hoping I might reduce the pain and stress of not knowing how they fared.

I also considered what I could do for LSU because I wanted to leave the school a different place from when I came. I thought of what John F. Kennedy, a president of the United States, said in an inaugural address: "Ask not what your country can do for you; ask what you can do for your country." Those words really inspired me. I wanted to give my service to this wonderful campus and its community, so I decided to play my part in student organizations. I wanted to bring diversity to each group and to bridge the gap between international and domestic students, and so help transform LSU.

One day, a group of my friends—who were from many nations and of many colors—were out together. A white gentleman came up to us and said, "Wow, LSU has come a long way." I looked at our group and realized how right he was. There we were, friends from Saudi Arabia, Ghana, Trinidad, India, Japan, and America. Yes, LSU had really changed from the days of segregation. Our group was like a little United Nations, and that's the image I wanted for our university.

I moved into positions of student leadership and became vice president of the International Student Organization, finding good favor and support among my peers and the faculty. And as I honed my leadership skills, always on my mind was the call to use those skills too in some capacity back in Africa.

14

CAUSE 4 LIFE

The school year passed quickly, and soon it was time to make plans for another summer. I thought back to the previous summer when I'd attended the Joni and Friends camp. During that time, through Sandy Hay, I learned that the Joni and Friends organization offered Cause 4 Life internships in California for those who wanted to learn more about their work. With such an internship, I would have the opportunity to learn how to serve the disabled and gain insight into a disability ministry run as a nonprofit organization.

But I had also been offered an internship in my field of economics, and such an internship would not only give me experience in my chosen field but pay me for my work. The internship with payment made sense to almost everyone. The problem was that I couldn't forget my conversation with Sandy Hay about interning with Joni and Friends. The dream God had planted in my heart was still there, and it was strong.

I contacted Sandy and asked about costs, time, pay, and location. She connected me to Rachel at Joni and Friends, who ran the Cause 4 Life internship program and who sent me the information about the internship. I learned not only that it was an unpaid position but that I would have to raise my own funds for it. That discouraged me, and the mental battle to decide which internship to accept went on.

I just didn't see how I could raise the money for the Cause 4 Life internship. When I expressed my concerns to the Cause 4 Life staff, they encouraged me to write letters asking for support. I had never done that before, but decided to try. I wrote about five letters that I sent to my church and a few friends. Within a week, I had raised the amount I needed for the internship.

That settled it. I was going to California. Some people thought I was crazy, but I was sure this was God's leading. I told the doubters, "I think God is going to make it all work out." Once again, I was grateful to God for his guidance in my life.

***

I arrived in Los Angeles very late—after midnight— then traveled north to a hotel near the Joni and Friends headquarters in Agoura Hills. I was overwhelmed by lights as far as I could see. A lot of traffic was still moving on so many highways that crisscrossed one another.

When I checked into the hotel, I learned I had a roommate. I opened the door to our room very quietly, trying not to wake him. But, of course, I did, and he sat up.

"Hello. I'm Michael, your roommate," I said.

"I'm Matija. Welcome."

I shared that I was from South Sudan and attending college at Louisiana State University, and he told me he was from Croatia and had a ministry encouraging kids not to do drugs.

"I was at a party with friends," he continued. "Then I got on a motorcycle, crashed, and damaged my spine. After I recovered from the accident, I got hooked on drugs. I was a mess until God changed my life."

"Wow. That's quite a story," I said. "I had tuberculosis in my spine and lost the use of my legs."

Then I told him I didn't know yet what I wanted to do with my life, but had been at the Joni and Friends camp in Michigan. I'd been amazed by what they did to help those with disabilities, and I wanted to learn more about the organization.

"I feel God can use me for his kingdom," I added. "Who knows? I might be president of South Sudan someday."

Matija laughed, but later he started calling me *Presidente*.

Sometime after our internship at Joni and Friends, Matija wrote a letter to Joni:

Though Michael and I are very different on the outside, on the inside he and I have the same spirit and hope in Jesus. He is destined to do something in people's lives. I learned from Michael that someone in a wheelchair can be a big influence—can make a huge difference.

***

The next morning, Matija and I met the other eight interns. We were all staying at the same hotel. After breakfast, we were picked up and headed to the Joni and Friends headquarters. As we drove through the beautiful hills, the sun rose, and I felt a new excitement about this opportunity.

As we entered the lobby, we saw a huge structure—a cross inscribed with the words: "But let justice roll on like a river, righteousness like a never-failing stream!" (Amos 5:24). I was struck by that display. I also still couldn't believe I was really here at Joni's headquarters.

We passed the large cross to find a "Welcome" sign. Everyone was expecting us, and they greeted us with joy and love. We felt as if we had always known one another, and soon we became one big family.

***

As part of our training, we went through a book titled *Beyond Suffering*, by Joni, Steve Bundy, and Pat Verbal.[2] The book is designed to help believers understand God's heart for people with disabilities and to discover how they can play an active role in carrying out the Luke 14:21 mandate: "Go out quickly into the streets and alleys of the town and bring in the poor, the crippled, the blind and the lame" (NIV). This training helped me think more deeply about the issues affecting the disability community

---

2 Joni Eareckson Tada, Steve Bundy, and Pat Verbal, *Beyond Suffering* (Agoura Hills, CA: Joni and Friends, 2014).

around the world and how I could respond to show the compassionate love of Jesus to them.

During that week, Joni was scheduled to come to our classroom to meet us and share some thoughts. She would be there for the morning and then have lunch with us. I couldn't wait for that time. I was so excited to meet her in person that I couldn't sleep the night before. It would be an honor to meet her as she had been a huge inspiration in my life. What would I say to her?

In the morning, we gathered as usual to be transported to the headquarters. While we would sometimes have to wait for stragglers to appear, that morning everyone was on time and waiting for our ride.

We were in the conference room when Joni came in accompanied by her husband, Ken. Her smile and joy lit up the room. We couldn't control our excitement. She said hello to the ten of us, greeting each person by name. I wondered how she knew me. Then I realized she had taken the time to look at our photographs and learn our names. That meant so much to me.

Joni shared her moving story. I had heard it before, but hearing it from her in person was much more powerful than seeing it on a video. I took notes, and here are some of the statements Joni made that touched my heart:

"God permits what he hates, to accomplish that which he loves."

"I realized that God does not take pleasure in my spinal cord injury, but he loves the way he is changing me in it and encouraging others through it."

"Psalm 10: God hears the cry of the afflicted. His heart goes out to those with disabilities."

"I do all I do because I want people to know the God I love."

"I would not trade this intimacy with God, this sweetness, this nearness, this tenderness, this preciousness of faith come alive in my life. I would not trade it for any amount of walking."

"God has not abandoned those with disabilities. No, he is working through them."

"God's power always shows best through weakness."

"The Bible says, 'Speak up for those who cannot speak for themselves . . . defend the rights of the poor and needy'" (Proverbs 31:8–9, NIV).

"That is what we are doing here at Joni and Friends. We are championing the disabled."

"We speak God's truth. Where the world is bleeding out of control, I want to be there. I've got a message to share."

When Joni finished sharing from her heart, she began to sing a hymn (which she likes to do). As she sang, I looked back over my life. When I had watched that video so long ago in the CURE Hospital playroom, I had not understood what she said because of my limited English. But even then, the video had made an impact. Now, hearing her in person, and because I had learned English, I was able to understand and I was left in tears. I was struck by her faith in God. As a quadriplegic, she had gone through chronic pain most of her life, and in the last few years, she had battled cancer. Yet her joy remained steady.

Only God could give that kind of joy, and I thanked him for bringing me all this way to meet Joni. I was stirred by her life's story once more.

***

"Being a leader is not about you, it's about the people you're serving."[3]

As part of our training, we worked through another book, this one titled *Lead Like Jesus* and written by Ken Blanchard and Phil Hodges. It's about looking into your heart and asking, *Am I here to serve or to be served?* And it's about understanding the vision, direction, and implementation of both leadership and service in your head. It really could be described as the process of aligning

---

3 Ken Blanchard and Phil Hodges, *Lead Like Jesus* (Nashville, TN: Thomas Nelson, 2008), p. 11.

two internal domains, the heart and the head, and two external domains, the hands and the habits.

The book is also about realizing that to really make it as a leader, you have to be a servant. And before you can hope to lead anyone else, you must know who you are. A lot of people think their self-worth is tied to how much money they make, how much recognition they get, and how much power and status they gain. But that is not who we are. Being a good steward is also key:

As a leader, you need to know how to be a good steward. You don't own anything. It's all on loan. So ask yourself, "How am I stewarding what's on loan to me?" As a leader you are a shepherd. Every human being is important and each deserves to be treated with love and respect.[4]

Servant leadership is all about love. It's about caring for people and making a difference in their lives. It's also about strengthening your inner person by making the habits of solitude, prayer, studying Scripture, having a small accountability group, and trusting the Lord's unconditional love part of your everyday life. Only then can you care for the needs of others.

Ken Blanchard's mother told him, "Ken, don't do good for other people to get something back. But when you do good, you're going to be amazed how much comes back."[5]

---

4 Blanchard and Hodges, *Lead Like Jesus*.

5 Blanchard and Hodges, *Lead Like Jesus*.

That book really impacted me as I was preparing to take over leadership roles on campus in the near future. From now on I would ask myself, *Am I doing this for me or for others?* The book became a guiding principle.

***

In addition to what I was gaining from the books we studied, I was gaining a lot of practical knowledge. I worked under the Wheels for the World department at Joni and Friends, learning the logistics of organizing a trip to send Bibles and wheelchairs across the world. This was the area where my passion burned most brightly as I remembered the images of my classmates at Masaku in Kenya crawling in the dirt to classes. I hoped what I learned would help me bring mobility to kids at Masaku and to many others in Kenya.

15

WRAPPING UP AT LSU

I had a new sense of purpose when I returned to campus that fall. Spending the summer with Joni had inspired me to press on, and I settled into my final year with a packed schedule. I was into my upper-level classes in economics, and they required a lot of study. On top of that, I was serving as the president of International Students and as executive director of Student Outreach in the student government. I had also recently joined Delta Sigma Pi, a professional business fraternity.

As president of International Students, I helped welcome and acclimate fellow international students, answer their concerns, and advocate for their needs to the university administration. I worked not only to integrate them but to help them share their beautiful and diverse cultures. As part of that, we celebrated an event called International Fusion, where international students could share their food, experiences, and native cultures with both foreign and domestic university students. The event drew a lot of attention on campus and in the community. It grew so large that we moved it to the Student Union

Theater, where we could better accommodate the growing crowd of participants.

As director of Student Outreach, it was my job to reach the multiple clubs and organizations on campus, helping and encouraging them to thrive. I listened to their concerns and represented them to the student government. Our goal was to better students' lives on campus.

All these roles helped me interact with a lot of students, and at the same time they gave me access to faculty and administration. I had opportunity to work closely with F. King Alexander, the president of the university, and also with Dr. Richard White, dean of the College of Business. These people—especially Dean White but also countless others—invested in me and poured into my life. They were always there to help me. Through their encouragement, God fueled my dreams. My motto became "Learn, live, and grow": learn through the Bible, live as an example of Christ, and growth will be the result.

***

During my last year, I wanted to do something for the campus that would make a permanent change. I remembered that Joni had quoted Proverbs 31:8 (NIV): "Speak up for those who cannot speak for themselves." I thought this was true for so many of those with disabilities, and that if I could help the 1,836 disabled students on campus, I would make LSU a better place.

I reached out to other students to form an organization for those with disabilities—the Disability Student

Organization (DSO). Its purpose was to bring awareness to all the students and to give those with disabilities a place to voice their concerns.

The questions and concerns put forth were eye-opening. Some had encountered the same issues I had with campus accessibility—problematic doors, sidewalks, and elevators. They, too, had difficulty trying to get in to see a professor or counselor. They, like me, couldn't just zoom right in as other students did. There was no equal opportunity for everyone.

My friend Sean told us about a professor who didn't want to let him make up a midterm exam even though he missed it only because his chair broke and could not be repaired for two weeks. He said the professor "was very belittling and rude to me and to the disability department. We believe a lot of professors just don't understand."

After we formed the organization, we saw a huge change on campus. People with disabilities were embraced and seen as equal members of the campus. It was a beautiful sight to see, but there was much more to be done.

***

In September, as President of International Students I was asked to speak at World Peace Day, also known as International Peace Day, at the Louisiana State Capitol in Baton Rouge. This was the first time I had ever been to a government event. Government representatives and senators, as well as representatives from all the universities and colleges throughout the state of Louisiana, were present.

As I waited to speak, I was a little nervous. Then when it was my turn, I could feel cold sweat on the right side of my face. I wiped it away as I proceeded to speak from my heart.

I started out by saying, "I'm from South Sudan, the youngest nation in the world. It is a country that has gone through many years of civil war. The war left millions dead and millions more displaced." There was silence in the room; you could hear a pin drop. People were thinking deeply. For me, this was a huge moment, as I had never shared such details of my background before. I didn't like to think back to those sad memories. I went on to talk about the greatest treasure humanity can have—peace.

Afterward, many of the audience came to shake my hand and tell me they were deeply moved.

***

Slowly, through my involvement on campus and through meeting Joni and Matija, I began to gain a vision for what was possible. For both Joni and Matija, their disabilities had meant significant personal loss and limitations. Yet God had used them because they *were* people with disabilities. I believed this could be true for me as well. Also, I once again saw that my education was not just for my benefit; it was for others who needed encouragement and an opportunity to succeed. The call of God was on my life; I had a great opportunity to serve him. I began to pray for clarity and wisdom.

When Joni and Friends proposed making a video about my story, I was reluctant at first. I had always tried to avoid the exhibition of my disability. I wanted to be viewed as normal Michael, a capable, educated man who happened to need a wheelchair. It took me a bit of time to come around, but eventually I thought, *This is God's story uniquely for me. There is not another story like it. Perhaps I should share it. Perhaps it will help or inspire someone to do what God is calling them to do.* So I agreed to let Joni and Friends film my story and share it around the world. After all, I had come to trust this organization and its people. I flew out to California for a couple of days to do the taping.

After the videotaping and World Peace Day, I felt a little more comfortable talking about myself. I began to have more opportunities to share my story in public, and I was finally able to deal with my perception that others thought less of me.

***

As I wrapped up my time at LSU, I received the surprise of my life. I was nominated to be part of the homecoming court. Homecoming is a huge annual celebration that brings together a whole school, including alumni. Part of the celebration is the selection of a homecoming court. Those nominated are students who have played a positive role either through service or leadership, and being selected is a huge honor and instills school pride.

The student body then chooses the homecoming king and queen from the senior class.

Most of the time those selected are the well-known, the beautiful, the handsome, the life of the party . . . and then there was me. Me? On the homecoming court? I could not see myself in that role. Then I learned that a lot of people had nominated me. At first I thought, *What do I know about being on the homecoming court?* But I wanted to learn about it, so I went to a homecoming forum. I then decided, *OK, why not? Let me give it a shot. Hopefully, it will open a door for the other people who don't feel comfortable applying for or who don't have the courage to participate in homecoming. I'm an international student, and not many international students do homecoming—let alone one in a wheelchair.*

Having agreed to accept my nomination, I applied and went through the selection process. Three senior girls were selected, and I was one of the three senior guys. The king and queen chosen by the student body would be announced at halftime during the homecoming game at Tiger Stadium. A lot of activities led up to that game, and I was so humbled to be part of the homecoming court.

***

All the court members woke up early on homecoming day as we had to arrive well ahead of the time for the parade. The day was beautiful. I dressed up in my purple and gold court clothes, then went to the start of the parade route to meet the others. A senior girl and I got to ride in a red Corvette.

We drove by University Lake, waved to the crowds who had gathered for the day, and passed out purple and gold beads—as was custom at LSU—to the people standing on the side of the road. The scene was unbelievable. I was smiling all the way.

After the parade, I went home to change into the suit and tie I had bought for the rest of the occasion. I invited Alicia, her kids, and two of my friends to go to the homecoming luncheon with me.

In the ballroom where the luncheon was being held, everything was beautiful, and everyone was dressed up in their best. The luncheon was attended by the previous homecoming king and queen, Miss Louisiana, our entire homecoming court, and many guests. Everyone was in a celebratory mood, and we greatly enjoyed the delicious lunch. I thought, *This must be the kind of food they serve the football players.*

We heard speeches from last year's king and queen and from all the other special guests, then took some photos and said goodbye to our guests before following the Tiger Marching Band down Victory Hill to the stadium. As we were going down the hill, it began to rain, and we took cover. I thought back to my culture where we believed rain was the blessing of God on an event. I looked up to the sky with joy, thanking God for blessing me on this special day.

Soon we entered the stadium and took our seats. Halftime came, and the court lined up in the center of the field, waiting to be introduced individually. As my turn came, a cadet pushed me across the field. I waved at the crowd, smiling from ear to ear as my image appeared on the jumbotron—giant—screen. I had been inside the stadium before, but never on the field. It was amazing to look up at so many people.

Then it was time to crown the king and queen, beginning with the queen. The announcer said, "The 2015 homecoming queen is . . . ." The crowd went wild, and the homecoming queen looked overcome with joy when last year's queen put the crown on her head and gave her a sash.

Then I saw the former homecoming king coming my way. I thought he was headed to the guy next to me. But at that very moment, the announcer declared, "The 2015 homecoming king is Michael Panther."

I could not believe what I'd heard. I was *stunned!* I could hear the whole stadium cheering for me. It was the same kind of cheer you would hear when the team scored a touchdown. I was so honored and humbled when President Alexander came and gave me a huge hug. He said, "We are very proud of you, and you deserve this award. You have represented our campus well."

As tears rolled down my face, I realized how far I had come. Here I was, a black, African paraplegic crowned and sitting on a stage before the entire stadium as they cheered for me. I had journeyed from the utter hopelessness of failed surgeries, homelessness, and starvation to a future full of hope. I had gone from the darkness and isolation of a tent in Kakuma Refugee Camp to this moment of great elevation. This could only be God's incredible work in my life!

***

Time flew by after homecoming, and I would soon be graduating in December of that year. It was time to take my final tests. I was looking toward the future. Where would God lead me? I trusted him fully. He still holds my future, and I still trust him!

I passed my exams, and so would definitely graduate. This was a moment I never thought I would have. I was very grateful to have reached this great milestone and excited for the next chapter of my life. It had been a miracle journey that I could not find words to describe. I know for sure it would have been impossible without God and the wonderful Mead family he brought into my life. They gave me hope, made me believe in myself, and saw so much positivity in my life. Now I was able to look forward to a better future.

The Meads came from the Philippines, where they were serving as missionaries. They couldn't miss this momentous occasion in my life. It was another beautiful day in Louisiana when they picked me up along with my brother, Ben Mead, and his wife, Laura. Alicia and her kids were there as well. We went to the basketball arena for the ceremony, and I joined the rest of the graduates all dressed in purple gowns.

After the speeches, it was time to receive our diplomas. When it was my turn, the whole crowd was super exuberant as people cheered me on. On stage, Dean White gave me a huge hug and celebrated with me. It was truly a humbling experience. I was thankful for LSU giving me three and a half wonderful years filled with experiences that shaped me. This school had wholeheartedly embraced me, and I rose from an invisible international student with disabilities to homecoming king. Being accepted by the students and faculty allowed me to rise to positions of leadership on campus. While here at LSU, I had matured in my faith and gained confidence. Its exposure to broader ideas and world perspectives had given me a new and expanded view of what the future could hold for me. I could never thank my professors and friends enough for the huge part they played in my life. These memories will live forever.

16

THE PATH FORWARD

Day after day, my desire to serve people with disabilities grew. I knew, however, that a structure above the ground—including any ministry—is only as strong as the foundation beneath. I wanted any ministry to bring mobility, and so to lift people out of the dirt and give them dignity, in Kenya and the rest of Africa, but I had to trust God and wait for his timing.

I had been offered a job with the Department of Economic and Policy Research at LSU in Baton Rouge, to begin after I graduated, and I was grateful to Dean White for connecting me with this opportunity. So after I spent Christmas at home in Michigan, I returned to Baton Rouge.

That first weekend back, Alicia invited me to her church. The pastor's sermon was titled "Building a Dream." What he said was a profound revelation to me, and I still remember it. He talked about Nehemiah who, though he was working at the palace at Susa in Persia, had heard about Jerusalem, and he was sad—so sad—about her plight. Nehemiah had a huge burden for the people he had never seen and a city where he had never been. Nehemiah's grief was so great that King Artaxerxes asked him, "Why does your face look so sad?" (Nehemiah 2:2, NIV). Nehemiah explained his people's situation and that he desperately wanted to rebuild the city of Jerusalem. He had a passion for the task.

The pastor then talked about how God's dreams start with a passion he plants in the heart of his child, a passion that often comes out of a burden. I realized that my deepest passion had been born out of my deepest suffering. And like Nehemiah, I had to pray until God positioned me for the task. When the time was right, God gave Nehemiah the courage to ask the king for what he needed. Then Nehemiah had to wait until everything was in place. Waiting was not wasted time. God was preparing Nehemiah, just as I realized he was also preparing me. In my heart I felt ready to go, but while I waited to see how my vision could be done, the key word God gave me was *patience*.

I prayed, *If you want me to do this, I have the passion, and now I am praying that you will give me patience.* But God had already put in place his next plans for me.

***

A few weeks before I graduated, Joni and Friends had invited me to attend their annual President's Weekend, where they would be showing the video about my life. As it played, I watched my image on the big screen for the first time, then turned my gaze to the audience.

Each person there was totally focused on my words. I saw that God could use my story to inspire others. In the audience that day were prominent supporters of Joni and Friends who were moved by my testimony—and who would become committed partners with me in the near future.

After they showed the video, I was interviewed by Steve Bundy, senior vice president at Joni and Friends. I shared what God was putting in my heart.

"What are you doing after graduation?" he asked me.

"I don't know yet. I'm waiting on the Lord. I know if I am patient, the Lord will work and open the right doors for me."

At that moment, Brian Boomsma stood and said loudly enough for everyone in the room to hear him, "Hired!" Everyone laughed, but Brian was serious. At the break, he came to me and said, "I'm the one who called out, and I'm serious. Can we have lunch together?"

Brian was full of energy—a true American entrepreneur. He was always thinking one step ahead of everyone else. I had known his wife, Mariellen, for three years, since that first Joni and Friends camp in Michigan. She had become like a mother to me—one of lots of mothers God has blessed me with. But this was the first time I had met Brian.

He continued, "If you want to, you can come to Chicago and work for me. Can you drive?"

Drive? No, I couldn't drive, and what's more, I didn't think I could afford a car with hand controls.

"No, I don't drive yet," I told him. "After I graduate, I'll have to take driving lessons and figure out how to get a car."

He said, "OK. After you learn how to drive, let me know."

I took Brian's words seriously. I now had an assignment that would further my dream—learning to drive. I tucked Brian's invitation into the back of my mind.

***

When I was back in Baton Rouge for my new job, I researched how to drive with hand controls. Realizing it was something I could do, I found an instructor. First, I took the written driver's test. Next, I had to work on actually driving, and I was excited to begin. When I got into the car, I thought I would just take off. But no, driving was *so* different from what I thought it would be. I drove in a circle. After one hour of "driving," I was disappointed by my lack of ability. Would I ever learn?

After my second time behind the wheel, I gained a bit of confidence but had a way to go. The instructor still had to brake for me, and I occasionally hit a curb. The third lesson was better: I got to drive in the neighborhood. When I had nine hours of practice under my belt, I could drive on the highway. Bit by bit, piece by piece, lesson by lesson, I did better, finally getting a pass to drive.

I contacted Brian and said, "OK, I can drive now, and I have my pass."

A few days later, he called with a surprise. "I really want you to work for me, and so I got a car for you."

I couldn't believe what I was hearing. This car would open a world of possibilities and freedom for me to do so many things I could not have done before. So many people had given me rides, and now I could return the favor.

A friend and I flew to Chicago, picked up the car, and headed back to Louisiana. As the hand controls were installed, I started driving.

Now I was ready to accept Brian's invitation to work for him at Dutch Farms, a grocery distribution company in Chicago where he was the CEO. He had already done so much for me, and I was grateful. I also felt working with Brian would offer many more opportunities to start the ministry I believed God had called me to do. I informed Dean White about this opportunity. He thought this was a good move. So I packed my things and headed to Chicago.

When I arrived, Mariellen helped me look for and find a wheelchair-accessible apartment, and then she took me to Dutch Farms headquarters. Brian was out of town for a business meeting, so she was the one who introduced me to all the employees around the office. Everyone was very welcoming. The man who would become my direct supervisor told me to report back the next week to start work as a purchasing agent.

Brian knew my heart and passion were in ministry to Africa. He offered me the job until I could figure out what God wanted me to do, how to do it, and how he wanted me to go about doing it. I was so grateful that God had positioned Brian and Mariellen alongside me at this stage of my life. At Dutch Farms, I gained much-needed experience in business that would help me put a firm foundation under my plan.

Piece by piece, I started building the dream of serving people with disabilities in Africa.

17

THE BIRTH OF LIVING WITH HOPE

Some dreams take time . . . and patience. And as I continued learning patience, I began making connections with people who could get my ministry started.

I had to work through many details. First, I connected with a lawyer who deals with the incorporation of tax-exempt organizations. He said there would be a small fee to do the work. But I was concerned for my family back in Africa, having finally learned where they were and that they were in desperate need. So I asked myself, *Should I use the little money I have to incorporate? Or should I send it to my family?*

As I was thinking and praying about this decision, I read Psalm 9:18: "For the needy shall not always be forgotten, and the hope of the poor shall not perish forever." The verse gave me the assurance that God would take care of my family, and I decided to use the money I had to incorporate.

***

The next thing I needed was a name for the organization. The name we chose began with that verse God had given me as reassurance for my family and which had stuck in my mind: "The hope of the poor." Then on the Sunday before we chose the name, I attended The Moody Church in downtown Chicago where the pastor's sermon was titled, "Hope Changes Everything." The hope? Hmm. That is not just any hope. It is the hope deep rooted in Christ, and that hope changed my life. Why not call the organization "Living with Hope"? I knew God wanted all people, no matter how desperate their situation, to live with hope.

Then I needed a board of directors, and I reached out to people I knew. The first person was Rick Gerig. I had known Rick and his wife, Lori, since the first Joni and Friends camp I attended. They shared my heart for people with disabilities and for the poor, and they were the first to believe in this ministry. They encouraged me greatly, and Rick became the president of the board.

I also talked with Mariellen and Brian Boomsma about joining the board. Mariellen shared the same vision I had, and she had been a huge support since the first time I met her. She willingly joined us.

Dr. Jeff Haag, an ophthalmologist, with whom I had become acquainted through his wife, Cynthie, became the third member of the board. He and Cynthie looked at me as part of their family. When the Meads were not around, I would go to their house for special occasions. They treated me like their son.

I then reached out to Dr. Mead. Having him on the board added great credibility to the organization.

That completed the requirements for incorporation, and Living with Hope was born.

***

The organization just had a name, though, and there was still a lot to be done. Rick advised me that, for successful wheelchair distribution in Kenya, I needed to learn from the Joni and Friends Wheels for the World outreach. He and Lori were going to Peru for such a distribution. "Would you be interested in going with us?" he asked. They were part of the team that included mechanics and therapists. I started thinking, *I should probably go on a trip to see how Wheels for the World operates their distribution. This would be valuable hands-on training.* I would, however, need to save some money for the trip.

I also needed a visa to enter Peru. This was my first time leaving the United States since I had come as a student, and I had a lot of hoops to jump through with U.S. and Peruvian immigration. I didn't know if this trip would be possible, but somehow God was leading the way, and he would make it all work out. I knew he wanted me to go.

My visa came just before we left.

We flew from Chicago to Miami and then on to Lima, Peru. Having stayed overnight there, we took a small plane the following day to Chiclayo on the coast of the Pacific

Ocean. Saturday was set-up day. We rested on Sunday, and then on Monday we started distributing chairs. I was eager to get started. Some people who came were getting wheelchairs for the first time. My assignment was to give devotions to the team and share the gospel with the wheelchair recipients. I also served with the main mechanic, John Boland.

As part of being an assistant mechanic, I taught the kids how to wheel themselves around in their new wheelchairs. They would go up and down the hall propelling themselves and learning to turn. The looks on their faces were priceless. They liked racing with me, and they wanted to do it as many times as possible. They kept saying, *"Una mas. Una mas."*—"One more. One more." I didn't speak Spanish, but I learned those two words.

During my breaks, I talked with the local team about what goes into organizing a distribution like this one. They were very happy to share their knowledge with me. After that trip and talking with those workers, I was more confident that I could do the same. The trip to Peru became the model for my first trip to Kenya. I asked Joni and Friends if they could provide me with a shipping container filled with wheelchairs, and they agreed to my request.

I would, however, have to figure out how to get the money to ship the container. I also needed to put a team together here in the States and form a team on the ground in Kenya. That second team would help arrange for Kenyans with disabilities to show up to receive wheelchairs.

I was fired up to resolve any problems I could foresee. I was ready to put these pieces of the puzzle in place. I knew God was calling me to this ministry, and I knew he had the answers.

***

I thought to myself, *OK, I have incorporated the ministry, but how do I get people to buy in to my vision? People say they're interested, but when it comes right down to actually giving money, they are not.* Pursuing my dream was not going to be easy. I was young, inexperienced, and right out of college. Who would believe in me? But I learned that sometimes God is working in hearts even when we can't see it.

When I first told Joni what I felt called to do, her response had been positive:

> *That's great to hear. I'm encouraged by your vision. There's so much to do in the kingdom, so many hurting and suffering people. I pray God will continue to use you to make a difference in their lives. I know that you are well on your way, and nothing could excite me more!*

It was encouraging to hear those words from Joni. They inspired me to keep going.

One thing I learned from the trip to Peru was that to make such a trip, you had to plan eight months in advance. It was close to the end of October when we returned from Peru, and I began to think about putting a trip together for the next September—eleven months away.

If we had a solid Kenyan team on the ground to find, identify, and encourage those hidden people with disabilities, it would make my work easier. My first thought went to Francesca, my dear sister and great encourager from my days at CURE. Her husband, Peter, was also willing to work with us, as was Daniel, a fellow patient at CURE. They all agreed to be a part of this vision. Having these three was a *huge* blessing, and I was confident they would organize everything on the ground in Kenya.

***

A year after leaving LSU, I had settled into a church home in Northwest Indiana—Faith Church. I enjoy this church because they have a strong ministry for those with disabilities called Reflectors, and I love serving with them.

In November of that year, the senior pastor, Bob Bouwer, asked if I would share my story as part of the Christmas message of hope. When I thought about it, I knew I wanted my story to also be part of a greater purpose at Faith Church.

I videotaped my story and asked if we could have a wheelchair drive in the spring. I knew a lot of people out there had wheelchairs they no longer knew what to do with, and that there is no secondary market for used wheelchairs. If we could collect these leftover chairs, refurbish them, and ship them to Kenya, they would be life-changing for those in need. This drive would help us collect more chairs and replenish the supply of wheelchairs from Joni and Friends. Pastor Bob assured me the church would be all in to do a wheelchair drive. I happily started looking forward to spring.

I had a short video clip that showed the reality of life in Africa for those with disabilities. It was made by Larry and Darlene LaPlue from Tennessee, a couple who had sent a container of wheelchairs to Kenya in the past. I got a couple of minutes in the weekend church services to share this clip, and the congregation was moved. People went to their homes, garages, attics, neighbors, and thrift stores to find and bring in mobility devices. Soon the whole entryway of the church was filled with them.

Those who did not have a device to give asked how they could help. I suggested they give money for the container shipment. When it came time to send the container, I had exactly the funds I needed in the Living with Hope account. This was truly God's provision.

In May of 2018, we shipped our first container to Kenya. Larry and Darlene said it took nine months for their container to arrive, so I was a little worried. We had about three months to get our container where it needed to be. I started praying, asking God to ensure the container would be cleared through customs as soon as it arrived.

***

While the container was in transit, I began the process of putting together the team that would travel with me to Kenya. All the founding board members signed up for the trip. I was delighted when Dr. Mead said he wanted to come. "Having you will give the team more stability," I told him. Rick Gerig's wife, Lori, and Dr. Jeff Haag's wife, Cynthie, also decided to go.

Now I needed physical therapists. Mariellen convinced her friend Casey Belford to come. When in June I went back to the Maranatha camp to connect with those who had become like family to me, God provided again.

"I have a friend here," one of the volunteers said, "and I want you to tell her your story. She's going home tomorrow, but we might find time to talk to her before she leaves. Her name is Cheri Boliantz, and she's a physical therapist."

"Could you come to dinner at the Mead home tonight and bring her?" I asked.

They came, and I told them my story and about the vision trip I was putting together. I also told them about the kind of people we were looking for and that we needed physical therapists. Later, Cheri wrote me:

Dear Michael,

It is an honor to be considered by you for this great outreach!!! I knew that God was preparing me for something, but didn't dream it was Africa! That is one place that never entered my mind as a choice. It gives me fear!!!

Yesterday I sought the Lord and He answered my prayers with specific answers. He has been pursuing me through Bible verses, people, and closed doors opening. It is humbling that the very God of the Universe cares to give me such specific answers to specific questions. He said, "Yes, I want you to go with Michael and the team, and this is all My idea."

I boldly came before Jesus with three requests:

1. *I needed a specific Bible verse to confirm. He gave me two!!!! He gave me the very one that sent me to Wheels Trip Romania, and the very one that He gave me to send my daughter to Cambodia. That scared me. Wowzer!*

2. *When I saw the time the trip was scheduled, I knew it was a bad time to leave work—when all the kids I teach have only been in school a few weeks. But my boss said, "YES"!!*

3. *My husband isn't full of peace about the trip, but he said, "God specifically gave you the verses, so you must go."*

I am still in shock that God answered me so fast, as clear as can be!

Cheri Boliantz

Also at the camp was a therapist named Dave Beimborn, the father of four boys. He wanted to bring his ten-year-old son, Aaron, on the trip. Then Jim and Toni Huisenga from my church joined the team. Others who committed to coming were Matija, my friend from Croatia; William Johnson, whom I met on the Peru trip and who became my best friend and big brother; and Dana Croxton, who had served with Wheels for the World for several years. Before we knew it, we were up to sixteen people. I knew all these people were coming because God had touched their hearts.

I talked with CURE Hospital, and they agreed to host the team. Through contacts in Kenya, we invited Pastor Hudson of Kangemi, a nearby slum in Kenya, to join our core team there—Francesca, Peter, and Daniel. I was happy to have this team on the ground in Kenya.

The container arrived at the port in the middle of August after a few delays. I was still concerned that it might not clear customs before September 7. If it didn't, I might have to cancel the trip, and I might not have these same people as part of the team again. I prayed, *God, touch the hearts of the customs people.* To my surprise, the container cleared in one week. That just doesn't happen! When I got the email saying it had cleared, believe me, I celebrated.

Now that our wheelchairs were on the ground in Kenya, we planned our itinerary. We would be at CURE Hospital for the first three days, then move to Kangemi for two days. We would also visit Masaku, my old school.

Living with Hope was established as a ministry. We had shipped and received our first container of wheelchairs in Kenya. We had two teams ready for action, and we had an itinerary. Our planning was finished. Now it was up to God to make it work, because he is the ultimate planner.

18

RETURN TO KENYA

After years of planning, thinking, praying, and holding discussions, the time was drawing near to go to Kenya and serve *people* with disabilities. I had dreamed of this time. I had a team of volunteers who were eager to get on the plane and go do the thing God had called them to do—distribute wheelchairs and share the hope of Jesus Christ. And I had a team in Kenya just waiting for our arrival. The container had also cleared customs. As far as I knew, all was ready.

On September 7, 2018, most of the team gathered at O'Hare airport in Chicago to begin the long trip to Nairobi, Kenya. Cheri came from Ohio and joined us in Chicago. Two others from California were flying straight to Kenya, unlike the rest of us. Some of the team had been out of the country before, but not many had been as far as Africa. They were excited and nervous.

I was excited and nervous, too, wondering what might go wrong. Each of us had two bags of supplies, so there was a lot of luggage to check for the flight. We flew from Chicago to Frankfurt, Germany, where we had a long layover and wandered the airport for five hours. Some team members found a corner where they could stretch out on the floor and sleep. Some visited the airport shops. Others were on their phones. Then at last the time had passed, and we boarded our next flight.

Finally, after twenty-four hours of travel, we touched down in Nairobi close to midnight. The long journey was almost over, but not quite. I had made plans for the team to stay overnight in a guesthouse in Nairobi so they could arrive in Kijabe a little rested. I was relieved to connect with the Kenyan drivers waiting for us there at the airport. I was doubly thrilled to see my friend Matija, who had arrived from Croatia.

We loaded the vans and headed into Nairobi. Even though it was late, the guesthouse was ready. We were ready, too—ready to stretch out flat and get some rest. But though I was tired, I was so wound up I couldn't sleep. I started going through our itinerary in my mind. Did I need to make any changes? Was everything really ready?

The following morning, we left for Kijabe. Arriving at CURE Hospital was like coming home for me, and memories and emotions flooded into my mind. I had left Kenya in 2012—six years earlier. I was excited to be back to the place where God gave me a second chance at life. Excited to see the CURE staff. Excited to work with the team. Excited to see who would come looking for help.

I met with our organizers and got everything set up to begin wheelchair distribution the following morning. I wondered how many people with disabilities would come.

Many people with disabilities had accepted their lives of isolation, hopelessness, and poverty. Perhaps only a few wanted to change that. Maybe wheelchairs were not what they felt they needed. My mind was rushing everywhere.

That evening we had devotions. A friend of mine and Mariellen's, Marlys Iperlean, had wanted to come on the trip, but she was ill and her doctors wouldn't let her. She was a prayer warrior and spiritual mother to me, with a sweet and beautiful soul, and a great sense of humor. But she wanted to be part of the team, so she made some video devotions for us to view each day.

That first evening, the video featured Ryan Matthysse, the worship leader at our church. In that devotion, Ryan shared some verses:

O people, the LORD has told you what is good,
*   and this is what he requires of you:*
to do what is right, to love mercy,
*   and to walk humbly with your God.*
(Micah 6:8, NLT)

If you help the poor, you are lending to the LORD—
*   and he will repay you!*
(Proverbs 19:17, NLT)

Give generously to the poor, not grudgingly, for the LORD
your God will bless you in everything you do. There will
always be some in the land who are poor. That is why I am

*commanding you to share freely with the poor and with
other Israelites in need (Deuteronomy 15:10–11, NLT).*

The verses were a comfort to the team who had left their
homes and traveled thousands of miles to another part of
the world to help the poor there.

We were all up early the next morning drinking coffee
and chai tea. Some team members were outside looking
down the Rift Valley or staring at the monkeys in the trees.
These monkeys were either gray and white, or little and
black-faced. The species of monkey didn't matter much;
all of them were entertaining as they jumped up and
down. It was a glorious day for doing the work of the Lord.

Arriving at the point of distribution, we got right to
work. I should not have worried about whether anyone
would come; that first day, people wanting wheelchairs
flocked in. The team on the ground in Kenya had done
a great job getting the word out. A crowd had gathered
earlier that morning and was waiting for us to begin.
There they were, the young and the old, the sick and
the not so sick. Some had dragged themselves over the
ground. Some had been carried. But they all came looking
for hope. Team members cried at the raw need they saw.

That first day at CURE, Jim Huisenga helped an old
lady who was carrying her forty-year-old son. He had
never had therapy, and his body was distorted so badly
that the therapists could barely unbend him to get him
into a wheelchair. That moment, the whole team realized

just how great the need was here in Kenya. For most of the Kenyans who came, this was their first wheelchair.

For thirteen hours, the therapists and mechanics fitted the chairs to the recipients and taught them how to navigate. The wheelchairs were a miracle to them, but we would not have enough . We felt bad when we had to turn people away. What we had was like a drop in the ocean. It was not enough.

At that moment, I recalled a story Ryan told in his devotion, adapted from a well-known essay titled *The Star Thrower*, written by Loren Eiseley.[6] You may have heard it in one of several versions, but the same message is still there.

After a storm, a man was walking on the beach and saw thousands of starfish washed up on the sand, stranded away from the water they needed to survive. Convinced he could do nothing to save them because of their great number, the man sat down in the sand in despair.

Then he spotted another man throwing starfish back into the sea, one at a time. He asked him why. Didn't he know there were too many starfish to make a difference? The man threw one more starfish into the ocean, smiled, and told him it had made a difference to *that* one.

Ryan went on, "I think too many people feel so overwhelmed with the poverty and the needs in our world that they end up doing nothing."

---

6 Adapted from Loren Eiseley, *The Star Thrower* (Orlando, FL: HBJ; First Harvest Edition, 1978).

Then he said directly to our team, "Maybe you are feeling overwhelmed with all the needs around you and all you have seen. I just want to remind you that God is not asking you to do it all, nor is he asking you to do it all at once, but to simply make a difference one person at a time."

By the end of that day, we understood better what Ryan had been talking about. We could help only one person at a time.

On Wednesday, the hospital had a chapel service, and our team shared what God had been doing for us. A pastor there spoke to those who had come seeking mobility devices. He said, "Today, God has remembered you."

After chapel, the nurses and doctors and all the CURE staff hugged me, saying, "Welcome home, *Pantha.*" I lost it. I broke down and cried with gratitude for all these people who had cared for me, for the way God had protected my life, for the Meads who had taken me into their family, for my education here in Kenya and at LSU. There was so much to be thankful for.

***

On the third day, we went to Kangemi, Kenya. Kangemi is one of the largest of many slums in Nairobi, with about 100,000 residents of multi-ethnicity. We set up our clinic at a church where Larry and Darlene LaPlue had been some time before. The local team had learned some important things about chair distribution from them that was a great help to us.

When we heard about someone in need, we would often send a team member with a chair to bring them in. But this morning we heard a *shhhsp, shhhsp* as Chama, whom you met in the Prologue to this book, paused her crawling at the doorway with flip-flops on her hands and great big, worn-out pads on her knees. She had come from twenty kilometers away, probably by bus, then crawled the last part of her journey to where we were distributing chairs. Speaking to her daughter, who was about three years old, she looked this way and that, unsure of her place here.

Matija wheeled himself over to her, then placing his hand on her shoulder, he greeted her. He assured her she was welcome and safe here. With the help of a translator, our team jumped into action. After a short time, aides lifted Chama into a wheelchair. Her eyes lit up with joy and gratitude because she could now look straight into the eyes of the workers from a sitting position rather than staring at their feet as she crawled on the ground.

The volunteers smiled at her and began to teach her how to use the chair. This was her first means of transport, and it would dramatically change her life. Now she could sit upright rather than groveling in the dirt, and the chair would immediately lift her status in her community. Perhaps most important of all, her newfound mobility enabled her to better care for her child. That little girl immediately climbed on to the foot pedals for a ride.

At first, maneuvering her chair didn't come easy, and Chama struggled. But pulling his chair next to hers,

Matija guided her hands—backward and forward on the push bars—and she learned quickly.

As she practiced, team members came with gifts for her: wheelchair gloves and clothing. She immediately left the room to put the clothes on her little girl and herself. When she wheeled back out into the waiting room, the group gathered there erupted in applause and encouragement. Everyone knew what this moment meant to Chama's life.

This is what our work is all about. This is the reason we have formed Living with Hope. This is why we go halfway around the world to Kenya transporting wheelchairs and mechanics and therapists—to help people just like Chama.

***

I had planned for us to go to my old school, Masaku, on Friday. That was the place where God had put into my heart the desire to help others. Unfortunately, none of the two hundred chairs we shipped for this trip were the right size for children. I promised myself I would come back and bring many pediatric wheelchairs.

But we *would* give the children at Masaku a "great banquet." This special party was inspired by the story of a great banquet in the Bible. In Luke 14:13–14, Jesus said, "When you give a banquet, invite the poor, the crippled, the lame, the blind, and you will be blessed" (NIV). We would honor the Masaku kids with delicious food, music, dancing, and small gifts.

***

After three days at CURE and two in Kangemi, we set out to travel to Masaku. Long before dawn, I was awake. My mind flashed back to my time at the school. I realized the students now attending were a different group of children from those I had known there. This was a different generation. However, I was pretty sure the kids I encountered this time would look and act a lot like the students I had known.

We packed up the small gift bags we had prepared for each child, in them toys, T-shirts, and toothbrushes. Then we climbed into the vans for the two-and-a-half-hour trip to Masaku. We were traveling east, and it was morning. Up and down hills we went through the Rift Valley. It was beautiful to watch the shadows move over the valleys and hills as we drove.

On the outskirts of Nairobi is Nairobi National Park. If we kept our eyes open, we might see a leopard drinking at a pond or resting in tree branches. Cheetahs, giraffes, lions, baboons, wildebeests, zebras were all living here, and were perfectly at home within the shadow of Nairobi's congestion.

On our left was Kiberia, the biggest and poorest slum in Africa. Kiberia reminded me of Kakuma with its makeshift shacks and poor living conditions. It is almost impossible to imagine the contrast between the slum, the park, and Nairobi's skyscrapers in such proximity.

Our hearts were made heavy by what we had seen as we journeyed on to the east.

***

When we arrived at the school, there it was—the blue gate. As I stared at it, my mind went to the Scripture story of Peter and John arriving at the Beautiful Gate of the temple in Jerusalem. As they approached, a lame man—a man with disabilities—was being carried in so he could spend the day begging from the people going into the temple. When he saw Peter and John about to enter, he asked them for money.

Peter told him, "I don't have any silver or gold for you. But I'll give you what I have. In the name of Jesus Christ the Nazarene, get up and walk!" (Acts 3:6, NLT). And that is exactly what the man did.

We realized we didn't have a lot to give the kids. But we could give them the good news about Jesus Christ, and that was what really mattered. From that day on, to me the blue gate became the Beautiful Gate.

As we drove through the blue gate, I was trying to look at everything at once. It looked much the way I remembered. And this school still felt part of me. It was the place where I got my start in education. It was the place that gave me the passion and burden I had in my heart.

Years back, when I first went to the United States to visit, I saw how people with disabilities were treated. My mind returned to Masaku, and I imagined how the students' quality of life could be improved if only they had a little assistance. Just a little help could accomplish so much. Maybe I could be the one to bring them aid. Masaku was the root of the Living with Hope ministry.

The principal came out to greet us. I knew him, as he had been the vice principal in my days. We crowded into his office to sign his guest book. Then we went outside, where music was playing through loud speakers and tents had been set up for the occasion. We went to see my old dorm, my old bed. The bunk beds were still there. The place had been cleaned for our visit, but the same filthy smell still clung to the place. Most of the facilities were barely improved.

Some of my teachers were still at the school, and they came to greet me. Sometimes teachers grow discouraged, but seeing me moving on in life encouraged them. My visit seemed to give them motivation to continue their work. I told them, "Your efforts matter." Their work on my behalf had been successful, and I left them with renewed hope.

To the students I gave the message that "each person has a story. It's okay to dream. You are uniquely made. You are no accident. You are here for a purpose." I wanted them to know God had led me and brought me through my difficulties, and he would do the same for them.

The major event was the banquet for the kids. We organized the chefs to prepare the best food possible, and our team was busily involved in serving the food, pushing wheelchairs, and loving the children. I was amazed at how much the kids could eat. They piled food onto their plates, ate it all, and then looked for more. This was probably the best food they had ever had. Some of the kids were dancing with joy. Those who had wheelchairs were spinning in them. I was overcome by that moment. It was a happy and powerful time for all.

The day ended, and it was quiet in the van as we started back. The team was deep in thought, and so was I. It had been a joyful time, but my heart was burdened for these children. I hoped God would allow me to serve them and many more, praying he would allow me to expand this ministry of hope in Africa. My heart was burning. *This dream is bigger than me*, I thought. *I cannot do it on my own. Lord, I need your help!*

19

JOYFUL REUNION

The plane lifted off, taking our faithful team home to their jobs and families. I would be forever grateful to them for the time they gave to this ministry.

Soon I, too, would be airborne, on my way to see my family—including the one person I had wanted to see for so long: Mama. She and I had not laid eyes on each other since the moment Baba and I had disappeared into the forest fourteen years earlier. I was only ten when my father loaded me on to his back and set off for Kakuma Refugee Camp. Now I was in my mid-twenties; I had become a man. I also wanted to meet the young sister born after my departure, and my other siblings who were very young when I left.

As I shared earlier, Sudan became independent in 2011. Then in 2013, during my second year at LSU, the country became embroiled in a deadly civil war. Huge numbers of people were killed or displaced, and I had no idea where my family was.

I finally learned they had fled to an internal refugee camp in South Sudan, news I heard after making contact with Uncle Abraham. Their arrival at the camp was nothing short of a miracle. The journey involved crossing the Nile River, so they and many other people piled into boats to cross. Some of these were overloaded and sank, but God protected my family and they had made it safely to shore.

I then asked Uncle Abraham which country close to that camp would be a safer place for them. He thought Uganda was best. So I sent the little money I had at that time to Uncle Abraham to transport the family to a camp in Uganda.

Were they safe there? Yes. However, the camp was much as Kakuma had been, if not worse, with a sea of people, not enough food, floods, cholera, and malaria. People lived in tents and ramshackle constructions. The conditions were deplorable.

By the time I made this trip to Africa, my family had been in that camp for about three and a half years. I arrived in Entebbe, Uganda, late on Tuesday. A couple of relatives met me at the airport, and we took a taxi to a hotel in Kampala, Uganda's capital city, where I had arranged for my family to come. But I had made this plan only a couple of days earlier because I didn't want them to be disappointed if something went wrong.

I didn't sleep much that night as I tried to weigh everything in my head. The first thing I wanted to do was find an apartment where my family could live and a place where the kids could go to school. The next morning, I got into a taxi and rode around Kampala to locate an apartment.

I have traveled in some major cities in the United States and in Nairobi, but never have I encountered the kind of traffic found in Kampala. The Ugandans' major means of transportation are *boda*, taxi motorbikes. Smaller than a full-sized motorcycle and larger than a bicycle, these *boda* zip here, there, and everywhere, taxiing people and their loads of goods. And they are loud. They dash in and out between cars, trucks, donkey carts, and people walking along. My intrepid taxi driver plowed ahead through this melee of traffic.

After driving around for a few hours, I finally found an apartment that would meet my family's needs. To rent the place for two months, I used money that the Living with Hope team had collected just before they went home. I was amazed by their kindness in going the extra mile to help me get my family settled, and felt relieved when I had taken care of this need.

Now it was time to go see my family . . . to see Mama.

My heart pounded as the car rolled up to the place they were staying, and so many thoughts rushed through my head. Some of my siblings came out to meet me, their eyes almost popping out of their heads as I got out of the car. Here was the little sister I had never seen, Sarah. Then there was Elizabeth, whom I did not recognize as she was born only shortly before I left. Soon my younger brother, John, joined us, as did Martha *Adier*, born during the hard times in Sudan. Only one sister, Monica, was not there because she was now married.

I hugged them all and was overcome by the emotions of the moment.

Baba came out of the house, and I could barely recognize the tired, bent old man he had become. The years of horrific conditions in South Sudan had taken a terrible toll on him. Baba always wanted to rebuild what was destroyed in South Sudan. He had been a warrior and a guardian of his home and village during all the seemingly unending wars. But his vigilance and commitment left him in poor health. As I looked at him, I remembered those nights when we stopped in the forest and he told me stories. I remembered, too, all the time he was with me at Kakuma and at CURE Hospital, and then when I begged him to go home to the family.

I was glad my dad was here today, and I prayed God would help me take care of him for the remaining days of his life.

There was singing and dancing on the compound, and then there she was coming toward me: Mother. Mama. She looked around in confusion. "Mama, it's me. Your son. Michael," I said. She came to me, knelt, and embraced me. We were both crying, overcome by the gravity of the moment. The bond of love between a mother and a son—regardless of time and distance—is unbreakable.

I thought back over all the loss I had experienced—first my family; then my friends at Kakuma; all I had known and loved at CURE Hospital; the tight relationships I had built at Masaku; and finally my many dear friends at Hillcrest High School. Like Job, I had suffered loss and didn't understand why. But bit by bit, God had begun restoring all I had lost, and laying out his purpose and wonderful plan for me. My heart exploded with joy.

Now everyone was crying. I can't explain the joy I felt at being together again, or the sorrow I felt for all the years we had lost. But now we were reunited. I could reach out and touch my mother and all the members of my family. *Amazing! Wonderful!*

At last, my mother and I released our hug, and I looked around at the rest of the family. I could see scars on their bodies from the years of civil war they had endured. They had suffered both physically and emotionally during those difficult times, and I hope and pray they never have to go through anything like that again.

Finally, we gathered in a small room and began singing and praising God for his goodness and grace in bringing us together again. "Today is a day of joy," my mother said. "My son was lost, but now he is found." My family remembered and talked about those who had taken special care of me—the Meads. Mama was praising God for them. They had been my mother and father when my family could not be with me.

I tried to talk in my native Dinka language, but I had lost much of it after being away for so long. After my father left CURE to return home, I had no one with whom I could speak the language, and little by little it slipped away. Now I asked my uncle to translate for me.

That special time with my family went by too quickly. The following morning, we went to find schools for my siblings. Once decided, we bought uniforms and other supplies they would need. Then we showed them the apartment and got the key. At last, my family would be living in a structure on solid ground, not in a tent pitched in the dirt.

God is in the business of restoration and he had surely restored my family to me. King David put it well, so long ago, when he said to God:

You who have made me see many
troubles and calamities
    will revive me again;
from the depths of the earth
    you will bring me up again.
You will increase my greatness
    and comfort me again.
(Psalm 71:20–21)

I had now accomplished what God had given me to do on this trip, and all was well with my soul. It was time for me to go home to the States and get back to the calling God had given me to do: building Living with Hope. Our mission is to give mobility to those with disabilities in Africa, and to introduce them to the love of God.

There was—and is—so much to do as we *all* live forward in hope.

AFTERWORD:

ARE YOU LIVING WITH HOPE?

Strength for today and bright hope for tomorrow . . .
"Great Is Thy Faithfulness," by Thomas O. Chisholm

Hope—a short word with an unending reach. We all have many opportunities to despair, to lose hope. Many times I could have abandoned hope. But God rescued me, kept me for his purposes, and gave me hope. It didn't happen all at once. God's purposes unfolded through everything he caused me to experience. All he taught me is now at work as I serve his mission through Living with Hope.

The first time God saved me for his purposes was when I was a three-year-old child lost in the forest as my family fled warring soldiers. God sent someone to find me and take me to my parents, just before death would have claimed me.

Then I became ill. Yes, serious illness was a part of God's purpose for me. In my homeland, boys as young as eight were trained as soldiers to fight for freedom. I, however, was too sick to train for war. I was embarrassed that I could not go fight and make my father proud. But most of those children never returned home, and I am still here.

God saved me on the long journey from Sudan to Kakuma Refugee Camp in Kenya. There was danger all around Baba and me. Wild animals, storms, floods, war, and the gnawing pain in my back made me want to give up. But our heavenly Father gave us the wings of a small plane to carry us to our destination. Without that help, I am sure I would not have survived. God once again saved me for his purposes.

As we waited at Kakuma for medical treatment, we had little to go on *except* hope. Our hope was tested again and again as we waited two years for rescue. At the end of that time, I was sent to CURE Hospital in Kijabe for treatment. My time there was the hopeful beginning of a new life of purpose for me.

Throughout failed surgeries and my wanting to give up and die, God sent people with a message of hope. Among them were *Daktari* and Mama Jana Mead, whose hope was so strong they took me into their family.

Their hope led me to school and an education. Going to school and learning was a huge goal for me. I hoped they would be the key to a new life, and they were. The schooling I received laid the foundation for me coming to the United States and going to Louisiana State University. Attending college in the States was almost beyond what I could hope for. But God, who had a plan and a purpose for my life, made it happen.

Why did God choose me and not others? I don't know. There were so many moments of real pain, real doubts, and real struggle with self-pity. Do you recognize a universal need to wrestle with God, to believe God, and to hold on to truth in the face of the contradiction of one's reality? Over and over I found determination, perseverance, trust, self-acceptance, and hope.

All hope has its roots deep in the reality that God loves us and he is with us in any situation. I had learned to know Jesus as my Savior long ago when an elder in my village told me about him. When I asked Jesus into my heart and life, a seed of hope was planted. I knew in that moment I had a ticket to heaven no matter what happened.

Two Scripture passages became the center of my hope in the goodness of God:

We know that all that happens to us is working for our good if we love God and are fitting into his plans (Romans 8:28, TLB).

For I am convinced that nothing can ever separate us from his love. Death can't, and life can't. The angels won't, and all the powers of hell itself cannot keep God's love away. Our fears for today, our worries about tomorrow, or where we are—high above the sky, or in the deepest ocean—nothing will ever be able to separate us from the

love of God demonstrated by our Lord Jesus Christ when
he died for us (Romans 8:38–39, TLB).

God drives away fear and despair, and gives us the strength to bear life's challenges, because the gift-giver walks with us. Such hope empowers us to live each day with an assurance that the best is yet to come, because God is faithful and true.

I seek to honor God by pointing to the work he has done in and through my life, particularly through my experience with disability. This book is not merely a story of my achievements. It is not an example of one man's success through his own efforts. My life has been full of challenges and limitations. It is not the story of instantaneous healing. At the end of this book, you find me still in a wheelchair, yet full of the grace and favor of God. For he has promised and proven to me, "I will never leave you nor forsake you" (Hebrews 13:5).

For people with a disability, here is a competing narrative to what society or their own hearts tells them. In this book, you have also found the answer to this question: How do we trust God and what he says about us? You have walked with me as I offered insight into the evolution of my mental and emotional states. These were strengthened not only as I matured into manhood but also as I matured spiritually in my understanding of who God is and who I am in him.

We all share the need to know we are not alone and that God actively cares. He gives us power to hold on. He has us on a unique path that, for the one who lives for him, leads ultimately to him.

So, dear reader, do you have hope? A sense of purpose? Or are you overwhelmed by the chaos and confusion of our world today? Right now you can find hope that will last forever. God made our search simple by giving us a guidebook—a road map. The Bible says, "God loved the world so much that he gave his only Son so that anyone who believes in him shall not perish but have eternal life" (John 3:16, TLB).

If you want to have that everlasting hope that only God—through his Son, Jesus—offers, here's what to do:

First, realize that you have sinned and you need a Savior. Then believe that Jesus Christ is the Savior you need. Last, ask Christ to forgive your sin.

Accepting Jesus as your Savior is simple. Just pray,

Dear God, I need a Savior. I have darkness in my heart and life. I believe your Son, Jesus, can take away my darkness and give me not only light but hope—hope for tomorrow and hope for the forever part of my life. I ask you, Lord Jesus, to take this awful load of sin and darkness and despair that I carry. Come into my life and change me from the inside out, and give me hope for an eternal forever with you.

That's it. That's all there is. If you say this prayer, the rest is up to God.

The well-known hymn "Great Is Thy Faithfulness" reminds us there is "strength for today and bright hope for tomorrow." That is the life of hope for anyone in relationship with God.

JOIN US

If you know Michael, you know his heart is as big as his smile. You can't help but connect with him. I knew right away that Living With Hope was going to have an impact on many lives.

It's been an honor to be part of the leadership team of Living With Hope from our very humble beginnings in 2017. The team God has put together in such a short period of time is a testament to Michael following God's vision. The occasions that have come our way in serving people in Africa have verified God's hand in that vision.

On behalf of Michael and our entire board, I'm asking you to join us on this journey. Come to Africa with us! Help us distribute wheelchairs and other mobility devices and pass out Bibles to hundreds of people. Join us in supporting children with disabilities attend school, some for the very first time. Help us encourage pastors to have a heart for the most vulnerable and underserved individuals in their own communities. Participate in making a lasting difference in developing countries that need a helping hand. Your time, your talents and your treasures are needed. Join us, won't you?

To find out more about how you can help, visit **Livingwithhope.net** or **Hopemobility.org**.

Blessings,

Rick Gerig
Board Chairman
Living With Hope / Hope Mobility International

CONTACT US AT:

Living With Hope / Hope Mobility International
P.O. Box 9266
Highland, IN 46322
USA

ACKNOWLEDGMENTS

This story has been made possible by countless friends and family. Many people have journeyed with me through sorrow to joy, through physical pain to wellness, through a time of despair about the uselessness of my life to a place of hope and purpose. Please know that I am deeply grateful for the impact all of you have made on my life.

To Gwen Ellis, my co-author and editor, thank you for bringing this story to life. Somehow you were able to get inside my head and help me tell my story. You were able to envision the places and people I had experienced on my journey and bring them to life on the pages of this book. Again, thank you for helping me put my story so eloquently into words.

To Michele Bovell, without your hard work, this memoir would have not been possible. Thank you for listening to my story, putting together a timeline, and beginning the writing process.

To Jean Bloom, thank you for helping me with the initial editing and giving guidance when needed.

Thank you to Joni Eareckson Tada not only for writing the Foreword of this book but also connecting me with my agent, Andrew Wolgemuth. Joni, thank you for being a big part of my life. God has used you to change me and countless others with disabilities around the world.

Thank you, Andrew Wolgemuth, for seeing this story as worthy and for guiding me through the publishing industry. Thank you, Andrew, for your kindness and patience through this process.

Thank you to the amazing team at 10Publishing, led by Jonathan Pountney. Thank you, Jonathan, Lois, Julie, Pete, and the 10 team, for taking tremendous care of this book and bringing it to life. I am deeply grateful for your incredible work and for the opportunity to partner with you to share my story with the world.

To the board of Living With Hope: Rick Gerig, Dr. Tim Mead, Jim Belford, Mariellen Boomsma, Jack Vroegh, Dr. Jeff Haag, Amy Van Drunen, Jim Huisenga, Jodi Van Veld, Dr. Richard White Jr, John Boersma and Pastor Andy Nearpass. Thank you for all you do for the ministry and for your guidance through this book process.

To my beloved Daktari and Mama Jana Mead: I have dedicated this book to you because, without you, I wouldn't be here. There would be no story. Thank you for sacrificing your lives to leave everything behind and go to foreign lands to serve those in need. Your incredible work has given hope and life to many, and I am humbled to be one of them. Thank you, Becky and Tom, Ben and Laura, Aaron and Rachel, and Abby, for welcoming me to the Mead family as your brother! I can't thank you enough!

Please know that I am deeply thankful to my Baba and Mama for caring for me when I could not take care of myself on my own. Thanks to my uncle Abraham who cared for me on my journey to CURE.

Thanks to all the doctors and nurses at CURE hospital. You saved my life.

And most of all, I want to thank God for this life . . . for this story. With God all things are possible and my story is only possible because of Him. He redeemed my life and gave me a second chance. In the midst of great pain, God did a miracle and restored my hope, wiped away my tears, and gave me purpose. "Marvelous are your works, Lord!"